Preaching on Peace

edited by
RONALD J. SIDER
and
DARREL J. BRUBAKER

FORTRESS PRESS   PHILADELPHIA

Library of Congress Cataloging in Publication Data

Main entry under title:

Preaching on peace.

    1. Peace (Theology)—Sermons. 2. Sermons, American. I. Sider, Ronald J. II. Brubaker, Darrel J. BT736.4.P73   1982   261.8′73   82-10958 ISBN 0-8006-1681-2

9611G82   Printed in the United States of America   1–1681

Contents

4

Preface

People who love life have always longed for peace. From the blood of Abel to the promise of Micah, from the blood of Jesus to the present nuclear impasse, millions have died seeking peace. But sadly, eons of longing have produced little more than fear and frustration.

If America is to turn back from the brink of nuclear holocaust, the churches must join the search for peace. And if the churches in large numbers are to be united in a new abolitionist movement— to abolish nuclear weapons—the preachers of our land must issue the summons. Many have already done so. We hope that this volume will embolden others to join them, and their hearers to welcome and encourage the trend.

Laity and clergy alike have already noticed how Christians everywhere are rediscovering their calling as peacemakers. Whether marching in New York City or praying in St. Peter's Square, Christians too are crying, "Enough! The insanity of the arms race must stop." No longer the exclusive province of the "historic peace churches," peace has crept out of the radical closet and into the established centers of power and influence. Who would have dared to predict even five years ago that evangelists of international stature and archbishops of vast reputation would be leading the antinuclear crusade? Pastors, bishops, laity—all are today proclaiming the good news of peace.

Some of the most significant voices have contributed to this volume. Roman Catholics, Evangelicals, and mainline Protestants are united in the conviction that our Lord summons us to be peacemakers in a nuclear age. Whether veterans of the peace movement or relative newcomers, they all believe that peace in our time can and must become a reality.

Each of the contributors to this volume has willingly given his or her sermon without financial return. As editors we are grateful for their kindness and commitment to the cause of peace. Because of their generosity—and that of the publisher—the enhanced royalties from the sale of this book will go entirely to The National Peace Academy Foundation, Washington, D. C.

It is our profound hope and sincere prayer that this collection of sermons will further advance the powerful and peaceable kingdom of God.

RONALD J. SIDER
DARREL J. BRUBAKER

Message on the Nuclear Arms Race

JOHN CARDINAL KROL
Roman Catholic Cardinal Archbishop of Philadelphia

Fellow Citizens:

Your overwhelming response to the Interfaith Committee's "Call to Worship and Witness to Stop the Nuclear Arms Race" is an exercise in religious leadership and responsible citizenship. As religious communities, united in the conviction that human life is sacred, we are duty-bound to articulate the growing concern of an increasing number of our fellow citizens that nuclear arms and their use exceed the limits of legitimate self-defense, that nuclear war is a crime against God and man and merits unequivocal condemnation.

Our Witness reflects the growing opposition to the nuclear arms race on the part of professional groups, scientists—including physicists—of the American and the World Medical Associations and the World Health Assembly, federal and state legislators, and the majority of the American public. In a recent Gallup poll, 72 percent of the Americans polled favored a United States–Soviet pact not to build any more nuclear weapons.

As reasonable people we are opposed to all wars, nuclear as well as conventional. We are convinced that peace is possible, and that it is our duty to pursue—with all our talents and resources—a just and lasting peace.

Our pursuit of peace is not based on a naive utopian view of the world. Our Judeo-Christian tradition is eloquent about the vision of peace. But it is also realistic about the fact of war. Governments cannot be denied the right of legitimate self-defense, once every means of peaceful settlement in a dispute has been exhausted. But nuclear war surpasses the limits of legitimate self-defense.

[Delivered March 27, 1982, at the Interfaith Witness to Stop the Nuclear Arms Race, Independence Square, Philadelphia]

There is at times a tendency to discredit our type of antinuclear witness by saying that it is a fringe action of bright-eyed visionaries who ignore harsh current realities. Let it be known that we are aware of the Soviet's avowed and never rescinded goal of subjugating the entire world. We know that Khrushchev was not joking when he said, "We are going to bury you," and Brezhnev was serious when he told the Twenty-fifth Congress of the Communist Party that détente with the West is no encumbrance for Soviet expansion. We know the tragic record of Communist expansion in the world and in our own continent. We know the long record of treaties broken by the Soviet Union. We know that the neutrality of Afghanistan did not prevent its being invaded by Soviet military forces, that the neutrality of Sweden did not prevent the penetration of its waters by a Soviet nuclear submarine. We know that the efforts of the people in Hungary, Czechoslovakia, and Poland to be rid of subjugation to Communist rule were countered by military force and by martial law. We know, too, the buildup of nuclear arms by the Soviets to gain superiority.

Judeo-Christian morality is not lacking in realism. We recognize the right of legitimate self-defense, but this right is not a moral justification for unleashing massive destruction against innocent noncombatants. We advocate disarmament—not unilateral disarmament but reciprocal or collective disarmament, proceeding at an equal pace, according to mutual agreement, and backed up by authentic and workable safeguards.

Too long have we been preoccupied with preparations for war; too long have we been guided by the questionable criterion of parity or superiority of armaments; too long have we allowed other nations to dictate how much we should spend on stockpiling weapons of destruction. The arms race is not a secure way of maintaining true peace, and the balance of power is no sure path to achieving it. In fact, we must ask whether the nuclear arms race is itself a threat to security and whether nuclear disarmament might not directly enhance national security.

Why do we call upon all governments to end the nuclear arms race, to dismantle existing nuclear weapons, and to agree upon a program of mutual inspection? There are many reasons. The first is that human beings normally use the weapons they develop. Doctor

Henry Kendall, chairperson of the Union of Concerned Scientists, says: "The risk of nuclear war has gone up and will continue to go up unless there is a major change in direction." The second reason is that millions of lives are at stake. Doctor Howard Hiatt, dean of Harvard's Schools of Public Health, tells us: "The greatest misunderstanding of all is the belief that we could tolerate a nuclear attack in the sense of surviving it. We have not come to grips with the reality that medical science, as well developed as it is, could do *absolutely nothing* in the event of such a nuclear catastrophe." Fire Commissioner Joseph Rizzo, director of Philadelphia's Office of Emergency Preparedness, said last September: "I'm the first to admit that the city is unprepared for a nuclear attack."

The Soviet intercontinental ballistic missile Savage carries a one-megaton warhead that packs the destructive energy of one million tons of TNT—about eighty times the punch of the bombs dropped on Hiroshima and Nagasaki. Yet in the spectrum of Soviet nuclear weaponry the Savage is only a medium-sized missile! These missiles are said to be accurate to within 200 yards—practically a bulls-eye —at transoceanic range. When such a nuclear warhead explodes, it produces multimillion-degree temperatures and generates forces of inconceivable magnitude. At the center of such an attack—a center which can extend to a square mile or more in size—there is instant incineration, instant cremation. The nuclear blast increases atmospheric pressures from the normal 14.7 pounds per square inch to 34.7 pounds per square inch, flattening most objects on impact— including human bodies. The noise of the explosion breaks eardrums, causing deafness. Even the slightest glance at the fireball causes focal retinal burns and blindness. Heat and radiation sear through all exposed body tissues, opening the body to massive infection. In the wake of the explosion, winds of 500 or more miles per hour hurl humans and other objects through space.

Such a nuclear blast will destroy hospitals, kill many physicians, knock out electricity, evaporate or pollute water supplies, and render travel practically impossible. Decaying bodies and spoiled food will generate epidemic diseases. International teams of scholars associated with the Pontifical Academy of Scientists, acting on the initiative of Pope John Paul II, delivered a paper to world leaders on "The Impact of Nuclear War." It contained the following statement:

"Recent talk about winning or even surviving a nuclear war must reflect a failure to appreciate a medical reality: any nuclear war would inevitably cause death, disease, and suffering of pandemic proportions, and without the possibility of effective medical intervention."

At Hiroshima, Pope John Paul II said, "Our future on this planet, exposed as it is to nuclear annihilation, depends on one single factor: humanity must make a moral about-face." This is the purpose of our Witness—to make our position clear:

1. We are opposed to all wars, both conventional and nuclear.
2. We believe that peace is possible, but it must be pursued with the same energy and determination as is used in preparation for war.
3. We acknowledge the right and duty of governments to legitimate self-defense, once all means of peaceful settlement have been exhausted.
4. It is a primary moral imperative to prevent any use of nuclear weapons under any conditions.
5. The deterrent effect of nuclear weapons is only as credible as the resolve to use them if deterrence fails. The use of such weapons is immoral.
6. The possession of nuclear weapons in our policy of deterrence cannot be justified in principle, but can be tolerated only if the deterrent framework is used to make progress on arms limitation, reduction, and eventual elimination.
7. It is imperative for the superpowers to pursue meaningful arms limitation aimed at substantial arms reduction and nuclear disarmament.
8. The phasing out altogether of nuclear deterrence and the threat of Mutual Assured Destruction (MAD) must always be the goal of our efforts.

As religious leaders, we must resist the conquest of the world by a totalitarian system. We must resist tyranny and oppression by every human means. But we must not act in an irrational and suicidal way, thereby forfeiting the grace which God will otherwise give us to enable us to persevere. We share a common belief in God, his laws and commandments, and we acknowledge a common code of moral conduct. I pray that we may also speak with one voice, the voice of human conscience, in persuading our political leaders and decision makers to change directions, to make a moral about-face, and to ensure that nuclear war shall never occur.

As the late Pope Paul said at the United Nations,

"No more war, war never again!"

"In a Dark Time..."

A. JAMES ARMSTRONG
Bishop, Indiana Area—United Methodist Church
President, National Council of the Churches of Christ in the
United States of America

> The unleashed power of the atom has changed everything except
> the way we think.
>
> Albert Einstein

> [Christ] is our peace, who has made us both one, and has broken
> down the dividing wall of hostility, by abolishing in his flesh the
> law of commandments and ordinances, that he might create in him-
> self one new man in place of the two, so making peace, and might
> reconcile us both to God in one body through the cross, thereby
> bringing the hostility to an end. And he came and preached peace
> to you who were far off and peace to those who were near.
>
> Eph. 2:14–17

The poet Theodore Roethke once wrote: "In a dark time, the
eye begins to see."

But does it? In this darkest of times is the human eye seeing?
The preliminary report of the International Public Hearings on
Nuclear Weapons and Disarmament said:

> In the light of the evidence, we condemn unreservedly any strategy
> that implies or advocates nuclear war-fighting; a limited nuclear war
> could not remain limited. We do not believe nuclear deterrence pro-
> vides a stable or acceptable basis to peace, and we fear that the doc-
> trine of limited war only adds a new stimulus to the dangers. . . .
> Negotiations should continue, the SALT process [be] restarted, the
> comprehensive test ban completed, and the nonproliferation treaty
> transformed into a more just and effective measure.

But, where is the eye that can see this? Where is the voice that will

[Reprinted with permission from *Orientation* magazine, July 1982]

speak of it? Where is the conscience of the religious community? Where are the leaders to lead the way?

On August 6, 1945, a gigantic atomic cloud mushroomed over Hiroshima. Between one hundred thousand and one hundred forty thousand human beings were incinerated in one blinding flash. It was the most heinous moment in human history. Was it the beginning of the end?

Ten years later the science editor of the *New York Times* suggested that our "advances" in nuclear technology had made that first atomic bomb outmoded. He said that we now—and that was in 1955, more than a quarter of a century ago—had weapons that would make the Hiroshima blast seem like "the pop of a toy pistol."

In 1945 we had two atomic bombs. Today there are more than fifty thousand nuclear weapons deployed or stockpiled around the world. Thousands of them pack more than fifty times the wallop of the Hiroshima bomb. Every major city in the USSR is targeted. Every major city in the U.S. is targeted. Europe has been defined as a primary "theater" for nuclear warfare. In the event of a nuclear war it is estimated that there would be more than 100 million deaths in the Soviet Union, 100 million deaths in Europe, and 140 million deaths in the United States. But who is to say for sure? Nobody has ever fought that kind of war before. One thing is sure: once it comes, life can never again be the same.

Jonathan Schell, in his awesome and frightening series of articles in *The New Yorker* earlier this year, may overstate the case when he insists that a nuclear war would reduce this planet to a realm "of insects and grass." Who really knows? But his array of scientific facts and projections is convincing, his arguments devastating, and his scenario has the human race poised at the brink of "apocalypse now." Even the most hawkish of hawks would agree that a nuclear war would be holocaust. Transportation and communication systems would be destroyed. The fabric of society would be torn to shreds. The human family would be irremediably damaged. Life as we know it would cease to exist. The national secretary of the Moral Majority shouts, "If somebody asked me if I was afraid of the atomic bomb, I'd say I'd jump on it and ride it to Glory!" Well, that man's death wish is his own business. But no preacher, no politician,

no military Neanderthal has a right to impose such pagan religion
and primitive immorality on more than four billion human beings.

Today thirty-five nations possess the knowledge to manufacture
nuclear weapons. Already ten years ago the Ford administration
was saying that that number would be doubled by the year 2000.
The knowledge is plentifully available—not only to governments but
in elemental form also to sophisticated terrorists and crime syndi-
cates. That knowledge will not be *un*learned. But it can be policed
and controlled. The present madness can be reversed.

Four years from now the military budget of the United States
alone will approximate what all the military budgets of all the
governments in the entire world totalled only four years ago. The
bellicose rhetoric and radical increase in military spending in this
country are not deterrents. They only feed the flames of fear and
irrationality. They make more likely zealous initiatives and trigger-
happy responses. And there is always the remote possibility of a
nervous "accident" or a psychotic episode à la Dr. Strangelove.
Initiatives, responses, accidents, and psychotic episodes take on
ominous new meaning in the face of the ultimate threat of global
extinction.

In April of last year I attended the Conference on Nuclear War
in Europe held at the University of Groningen in Holland. The
speakers and panelists were military persons, diplomats, and scholars.
Drawing from official sources and statements made by the American,
Russian, Warsaw Pact, and NATO leaders and government agencies,
they documented the world's insane course. They expressed their
hopelessness and anger over the situation. Buttons pushed in the
Kremlin or in the White House could plunge the whole world into
darkness. It would be "annihilation without representation." A hand-
ful of superpower elitists could determine the "final solution" and
people everywhere could be burned to death, blown away, or reduced
to subhuman levels of existence in a matter of minutes. Small wonder
that there have been indignant demonstrations in Bonn, Rome, Lon-
don, Budapest, Scandinavia, and many other places.

The Christian community is also coming alive to the issue. In
February I lunched with Father Theodore Hesburgh, president of
Notre Dame University and citizen extraordinary. He told me of
his "conversion" last November. Father Hesburgh has been a voice

of conscience on many fronts. He has served on the U.S. Civil Rights Commission. He has faithfully served administrations of both political parties dealing with a wide variety of issues related to human justice and public welfare. But at a convocation at his own school last fall he said, "There is a reawakening of the human race to the fact that we are on the verge of blowing ourselves up." That convocation at Notre Dame was one of many such day-long meetings sponsored on 146 college campuses across the U.S. and Canada by the Union of Concerned Scientists. Previously, Father Hesburgh had committed himself to scores of righteous causes. Now he would focus on just one—*human survival:* Governments must stop manufacturing nuclear arms. Deployed weapons must be removed. Stockpiles must be reduced and dismantled. Proliferation must stop. The nuclear threat is qualitatively different from any other.

Nor does Father Hesburgh stand alone. Pope John Paul II has voiced his strenuous opposition to the nuclear arms race. The U.S. Conference of Catholic Bishops, led by Archbishop John Roach of Minneapolis, has declared itself unalterably opposed to the nuclear arms race. Archbishop Raymond G. Hunthausen of Seattle, in a courageous sermon preached last year, called for unilateral disarmament and nonviolent resistance: "I think the teaching of Jesus tells us to render to a nuclear-armed Caesar what that Caesar deserves—tax resistance."

Billy Graham stated almost three years ago:

> I have gone back to the Bible to restudy what it says about the responsibilities we have as peacemakers. I have seen that we must seek the good of the whole human race, and not just the good of any one nation or race. There have been times in the past when I have, I suppose, confused the kingdom of God with the American way of life. . . . But the kingdom of God is not the same as America, and our nation is subject to the judgment of God just as much as any other nation.

Even earlier, in a CBS interview, he had said:

> The people of the United States want peace. The people of China want peace. The people of the Soviet Union want peace. We don't seem to realize how these weapons are proliferating and that we're now spending $400 billion annually on the arms race in our world— insanity, madness! . . . I'm in favor of disarmament and I'm in

favor of trust. I'm in favor of having agreements not only to reduce
but also to eliminate. Why should any nation have atomic bombs?

Riverside Church in New York City is considered by some to be
the "cathedral church of American Protestantism." Led by William
Sloane Coffin, the church has become the center of a national
movement to "reverse the arms race." When I was elected President
of the National Council of Churches last November, I said that the
NCC must be highly selective in sorting out issues to be addressed.
It must give primary attention to those issues that are of "supreme
importance to the future of the human family." At the top of that
list, I insisted, is "the madness of the nuclear arms race."

I, for one, do not believe in the practicality of unilateral disarmament. That is not a present possibility. But I do believe in *unilateral
initiatives*—based on good faith and trust. Anwar Sadat made his
historic trip from Cairo to Jerusalem without announcement. It was
the most dramatic foreign policy initiative of recent years. That sort
of initiative, seized by a Russian chairman or an American president,
could open a door. Only God knows what might follow. But do our
leaders have sufficient wisdom and courage to set aside zealous
nationalism, political posturing, and ego for the sake of a human
future? In a dark time can their eyes see? Can they respond?

What is the biblical base for nuclear disarmament? It is found in
the messianic vision of Isaiah 9 and the prophetic assurance that
nations shall "beat their swords into plowshares, and their spears
into pruning hooks; nation shall not lift up sword against nation,
neither shall they learn war any more" (Isa. 2:4). That hope was
echoed in an angel chorus over the manger in Bethlehem. Our
response to and participation in the vision was spelled out by the
Prince of Peace in his Sermon on the Mount. When, at the last, a
devoted disciple tried to defend his Lord, Jesus said, "Those who
live by the sword shall perish by the sword." (Nearly 2000 years
later Albert Schweitzer would say in his famous Oslo broadcast,
"Those who live by the bomb will perish by the bomb.")

The cross stands central in any understanding of violence. It *must*
be applied to the possibility of nuclear annihilation. "Christ is our
peace, who has made us [historic enemies] both one, and has broken
down the dividing wall of hostility . . . that he might create in himself one new man in place of the two, so making peace."

But the cross does not belong to Christ alone: "If anyone wants to be a follower of mine, let that person renounce self and take up the cross and follow me" (Mark 8:34). That statement stands at the heart of Mark's Gospel. Link the cross, in your thinking, with Christ's commandment to love God and neighbor—including the "enemy." Our Lord fleshed out that teaching and was crucified. As his followers in this nuclear age we are called precisely to take up our cross and follow where he leads.

The theme of the oneness of creation moves as a demanding strand through Holy Scripture from the story of Creation to the fashioning of a "new heaven and a new earth." To embrace that vision in the name of Christ requires both faith and risk. Nuclear disarmament is a risk-taking venture. But how much greater is the risk forced upon us by a mythology that falsely names West "good" and East "evil," that insists human security can be found in a balance of nuclear terror or in "winning" an unwinnable nuclear arms race.

Jonathan Schell concluded his recent *New Yorker* article on "The Choice" with these words:

> One day—and it is hard to believe that it will not be soon—we will make a choice. Either we will sink into the final coma and end it all or, as I trust and believe, we will awaken to the truth of our peril, a truth as great as life itself, and like a person who has swallowed a lethal poison but shakes off his stupor at the last moment and vomits the poison up, we will break through the layers of our denials, put aside our fainthearted excuses, and rise up to cleanse the earth of nuclear weapons.

Is Peace Controversial?

CYNTHIA C. WEDEL
Episcopalian Lay Woman
Member of the Presidium, World Council of Churches

God was in Christ reconciling the world to himself, not counting their trespasses against them, and entrusting to us the message of reconciliation.

                                                                    2 Cor. 5:19

To a Christian who reveres the Prince of Peace it seems hard even to imagine peace being a controversial subject. The fact remains, however, that it is. The reasons for this are varied, some rooted deep in our human nature, others rooted in our varying ideologies and systems of moral values. Probably no sane human being would say that war and conflict are preferable to peace. But at the same time there is usually strong objection to the concept of "peace at any price." Almost all wars have been justified by those who wage them—however thin the justification!

As a psychologist I am especially interested in the personal, deep-rooted inner drives that form and uphold our attitudes toward conflict, aggression, and war. They constitute an important area for study because, in the last analysis, these drives are what "require" people to make war.

To look at our inner motives and pressures, I would like to go back to the biblical story of creation. I'm not troubled when people refer to it as a "story." No intelligent person today tries to prove that it is a literal description of creation. It is, rather, a profoundly philosophical and religious statement of one basic fact—*in the beginning, God!* Those who told the story, and those who eventually wrote it down, were puzzling over the *why* of things. There were

[Delivered June 1980 to the Southern California Presbyterial Assembly meeting in Claremont, California]

probably some people, even in those prescientific days, who thought that the universe and this world came into being as a purely accidental occurrence—an ancient version of the big-bang theory we hear about today. But there were others, even then, who said no: The universe and this world are too orderly, too carefully constructed to be simple accident. There has to be intelligence behind it—planning and a purpose. Even as a reasonably well informed modern person, I cannot accept the idea of no planning, no order, no predictability. Everything I see and experience, and everything I learn from science, convinces me that there *is* order and purpose. If not, there could be no "laws of nature," no predictability, no science. The Bible, the Judeo-Christian tradition, and the other great world religions all share the belief that there is an intelligence and a plan for the creation, and that the Planner is benevolent and loving.

But if this is so, why is the world in such a mess? Couldn't God have prevented much of the grief and turmoil which have marked all of human history? Again, the Genesis story gives us a clue. As the climax of the creation—on the sixth day—God created human beings "in his own image." Obviously, being made in the image of God does not mean that we look like God. But we do have some qualities which no other form of life seems to have—the ability to remember and to plan ahead, and to a limited extent the ability to create and invent. But the most significant factor is that God made human beings free. As far as we know, we are the only beings in the created order who are not totally bound by our instincts. We can choose what we will and will not do. We can refuse to obey God, and even deny his existence. It may well be that freedom is our most God-like quality—and also our greatest temptation. We constantly want to "play God"—to grab power and lord it over others. Our freedom allows that. Why would a wise and loving God do such a foolish thing as to give us this freedom? He could just as easily have made us with built-in instincts to do the right things—and thereby saved himself and us endless trouble.

The only reason I have been able to figure out for God's giving us this dangerous gift of freedom lies in God's own nature. Somewhere in the Bible there appears the phrase, "God is love." It's not just that God loves, but that—in some strange way—love is the absolute essence of God. If this is true, surely such a God would want love in his creation. But how do you create love? This must have posed a problem even for God. Love is not something to be formed like a rock or a tree. Love involves relationship. God knew this. He knew that if there was to be love in the universe, he would have to create a being capable of a relationship of love with the Creator.

But God also knew something which we often forget—that the highest form of love must always be an absolutely free gift. If there is any kind of coercion or force or bribery, it may look like love but it will not be the real thing. Therefore, if God wanted love in the universe, it was necessary to create a free being, and God would then have to woo and win the love of his creature. This, I believe, is why God gave to us humans the dangerous gift of freedom—not for our own selfish ends but for the glory of God.

It is interesting to look back through history and see how human beings, as soon as they began to acquire knowledge or wealth or information, used these gifts to seize power and lord it over others. The history of human life is the history of hierarchies set up by individuals or small groups who made all the rules and forced others to obey and submit. This has been the story of governments, the church, business, education, and the family.

Such inequality, such selfish use of power creates a perfect setting for conflict. This conflict is not limited to hot war and overt strife, but can be seen also in the competitiveness which is so much a part of human life. Even among humane and civilized people it is assumed that human beings are motivated only by competition—the desire to get ahead of others, to win. Our educational system itself is built on competition—getting the best grades, being at the head of the class. Children are often punished just for helping one another!

I firmly believe that it is this deep-seated, age-old indoctrination in the idea that each of us is out to achieve our own goals at the expense of everybody else which makes working, speaking, or demonstrating for peace so controversial. We assume that other nations, like other individuals, are basically hostile and will "get us" if we don't "get them" first. In the light of this, we Christians ought to have the most profound respect for the historic peace churches—the Quakers, Brethren, and Mennonites—whose people are pacifists and refuse to participate in war. They have suffered severely for their position. Most of the rest of us justify our militarism as pragmatic, or patriotic. I am as guilty as anyone else in this respect—and ashamed of it.

The human tendency to compete, to win, to gain power has been with us throughout history. But today we are living in a world where the dangers of war and the possibilities of peace are greater than they have ever been. I am convinced that you and I—ordinary citizens of one of the "great powers" in our world—have an enormous responsibility to try to understand what is happening, and to find ways in which we can contribute to peacemaking.

One of the major changes in our time has been the development of rapid transportation and almost instantaneous communication on a worldwide basis. These technological changes have caused our world to shrink from a very large, mostly unknown place to an intimate little global village. We can sit in our own comfortable TV rooms and see people living and dying on the opposite side of the world. We are aware, almost as it happens, of every disaster or calamity that occurs anywhere. When people complain—as they often do—about the fact that there are too many awful things happening these days, I remind them that such things have always happened, but in earlier eras we didn't know about them—or we heard of them only months or years later.

The transportation and communication revolution also means that people in far-off places like Asia and Africa know a great deal about us and how we live. This knowledge has brought a rising tide of expectations to people who have known nothing but grinding poverty, illiteracy, and disease. This is why we read so much today about uprisings and revolutions. People start revolutions only when they begin to have hope for a better life.

We in the West find many of the changes in our world today uncomfortable. We wish we could go back to the "good old days" when people knew their place and stayed in it.

But as Christians we have to ask ourselves: "What may God be saying to us in all of this? What does God want?" I feel sure that the God who made and loves us made and loves also every one of his human children. I suspect that the long ages during which a small segment of the world's population had all the knowledge, wealth, and power were not what God wanted. God is infinitely patient, but I see—even in all the turmoil of today—God beginning to open opportunities for a good life to all people everywhere. Communication is a part of this. As we get to know people in other parts of the world, we discover that they want the same things we want. I believe increasingly that God's will for his world is that someday we will all know and respect one another and learn to share the resources of the planet, and to take care of it as our common home.

I also deeply believe that God cares about every one of his human children, and wants for every one a chance for a decent life, enough food, medical care, and the opportunity to develop one's own abilities and talents. I find it breathtaking to think that you and I are living in the first generation in human history where this begins to be possible.

After an assessment of the vast changes in our world, we need to look at the clashes of ideologies in our time—made more vivid by our rapid communications. One of the largest of these clashes is that between Communists and anti-Communists. All of us are aware of how much this rivalry makes the headlines, and how often we are told that our country must do one thing or another in order to "combat Communism." I am not a Communist, and I have no use whatsoever for the Communist form of government or way of life. But I believe that there are many people in our world, even in our country, who find it to their personal advantage to keep the fear of Communism alive. Actually, Communism has failed, but we as a nation do not seem to realize that fact or take advantage of it. Any government that feels compelled to maintain a police state, and refuses to let its citizens leave the country, is obviously not a government "of and by the people." A truly democratic society—such as our own with all its faults—is infinitely stronger than such a police state. Those who foster a hysterical fear of Communism, and the arms race that is based on it, do a great disservice to all of us. In talking with Russian Christians (who dislike Communism far more than we do because they suffer from it daily), I have found that they are given the same kind of propaganda we are: they are told they must sacrifice for greater armaments because their adversary is so far ahead of them in its military buildup.

In the World Council of Churches, where Christians from all nations and ideologies can meet and share as Christians, one gets a picture of the world that is very different from the one we get in the newspapers back home. I recall how vigorously people in this country reacted to a WCC grant to some Black Africans a few years ago. Many of the recipient Black churches were members of the WCC. We knew their people well. We knew they were not Marxists, but patriots trying to free their homeland. We have since learned that this WCC action was blown up for propaganda purposes by the white government ruling Rhodesia at the time. When the British government finally stepped in and brought about the present hopeful settlement in what is now Zimbabwe, we felt that our actions had been vindicated.

Indeed, I am coming to believe ever more strongly that the modern ecumenical movement, including the World Council of Churches, may be one of the means God is trying to use to make his will known. It seems significant that God inspired many of the churches to send missionaries to Asia, Africa, and Latin America just at the dawn of this century, when so many great changes were about to occur. If God is indeed pushing and pulling us toward one world of peace and brotherhood, he may have been using his church as the forerunner for the rest of the society. Within this century, strong Christian churches have been developed in every part of the world. Almost all of them share in the ecumenical movement—even the vast Roman Catholic church. It has not yet joined the WCC, but there are many areas of common activity and close cooperation.

In the view of people who are terribly afraid, those who believe what the "fearmongers" in our own country and other countries are saying, we who see hope in the present world are often accused of being either naive or actually subversive. But to us the dream of "one world" is a dream we believe God has implanted. The fact is that most Christians in the U.S. are not only hopeful; we are also patriotic Americans. We believe in our country and in our form of government and we are not afraid of inroads being made by so-called subversives. We want our country to give the world the moral leadership it is capable of giving. That means we don't want it to base all our national decisions on a fear of other ideologies—or on "profits."

The idea that the only way we can be safe is to have more nuclear weapons than everybody else is suicidal. (It is also bad for the economy.) There is strong evidence that God is still at work—shrinking the world, raising up great leaders in many of the developing countries, stimulating new discoveries and inventions that can help to provide for the needs of everyone.

The word *reconciliation* is a good biblical word. In Corinthians we read: "God was in Christ reconciling the world to himself . . . and has entrusted to us the ministry of reconciliation." As American Christians you and I can be agents of reconciliation. All we need is to be well-informed, articulate, loyal Americans—and to really believe and trust in God.

An Evangelical Witness for Peace

RONALD J. SIDER
Associate Professor of Theology,
Eastern Baptist Theological Seminary, Philadelphia

It is no longer I who live, but Christ who lives in me.
Gal. 2:20

I am honored to be here as President of Evangelicals for Social Action, a national movement of evangelical Christians committed to stopping the nuclear arms race.

I am also honored to be here as an evangelical Christian. We all know that some highly visible and vocal evangelical leaders support President Reagan's massive military buildup. Among evangelical Christians, however, they do not represent a majority. Most evangelical Christians are proud of Billy Graham's courageous peace pilgrimage to Moscow in spite of vigorous opposition from the U.S. State Department. More and more evangelical Christians are coming to the conclusion that nuclear war can never be justified. In fact, President Reagan's pastor, the Rev. Donn Moomaw of Bel Air Presbyterian Church, said in a recent sermon: "Because nuclear weapons are so destructive, so devastating, so final . . . they are morally indefensible. I must be a nuclear pacifist."

I am honored to be here, finally, as a citizen of our diverse, pluralistic society. We come together today as Baptists and Buddhists, Catholics and charismatics, Jews and Jesuits, humanists and Hindus, Muslims and Methodists—to say no to nuclear madness. Each of us has our own way of explaining why our deepest beliefs compel us to oppose the arms race. Because we respect each other's different traditions we need to share with each other the diverse bases of our

[Delivered in slightly revised form June 6, 1982, at Peace Sunday, an interreligious peace rally to protest the nuclear arms race, held in the Rose Bowl, Pasadena, California]

25

common concern for peace. Briefly, then, permit me to share why I as an evangelical Christian believe that a decision to continue the nuclear arms race would be one of the most immoral decisions in history.

Christians believe that the good earth, all life, and you and I are the creation of a personal, loving God. We do not believe that persons and nature have resulted from the accidental combination of subatomic matter in a blind materialistic process. If that were true, persons would merely be complex machines, and ethical values— even with respect to peacemaking—would be totally subjective products of blind chance. Certainly the Creator used a gloriously complex evolutionary process stretching over vast geological ages to create the world. But it was not an accident.

The Almighty Creator is an Infinite Person who wants to be in free, loving relationship with finite persons. So the Creator molded you and me in the divine image. *That* is why I believe that every person is of infinite value. The worth of individuals does not depend on their productivity or usefulness to society. Every person is created in God's image for personal relationship with the Lord of the universe. *That* is why it is wrong for totalitarians to sacrifice millions of people for the alleged benefit of the state. *That* is why it is wrong for American and Russian militarists to build megaton weapons that will destroy people by the hundreds of millions.

Not just persons but the earth itself also comes from the Creator's loving hand. As I worked on my book *Nuclear Holocaust and Christian Hope,* my love for the gorgeous beauty of the earth grew deeper and deeper. As I faced the stark reality that human madness might actually destroy our little planet in my lifetime, I fell more deeply in love with the soft gentle breezes, the majestic redwoods, and the purple sunset. Christians believe that the earth is a ring from the Beloved to be cherished and preserved, not an accidental commodity to be exploited and destroyed. To continue down a path that makes nuclear destruction ever more likely does not merely reflect callous contempt for future generations; it also demonstrates a blasphemous affront to the Creator of this gorgeous, fragile planet.

The Creator intended persons to live together in harmonious human society shaping cultures and civilizations of beauty, justice, and peace. But human history is a tragic mixture of good and evil. So often human greed, national pride, and sheer selfishness have led to ghastly conflict. Choosing to deny that we are made for obedient relationship with God, choosing to love ourselves more than our neighbor, we have created an upward spiral of violence. Clubs have given way to cannons; firebombs to 20-megaton nuclear warheads. Today we stand trembling at the precipice, peering fearfully into the nuclear abyss.

Still, my friends, I have hope. I believe that it is possible to obtain nuclear disarmament within the next twenty-five years. The basis of my hope, however, is not primarily the growing antinuclear movement, although I am deeply involved in and highly grateful for that movement. The basis of my hope is God.

Christian faith reminds me that God has taken the initiative to correct all that is evil and unjust in the world. Christians believe that the Creator of the galaxies actually took on human flesh and walked the dusty paths of Palestine as a humble teacher. He taught that we should be peacemakers and love our enemies. He cared for the poor and the weak, the sick and the social outcasts, those whom the powerful always ignore. He said that God loves even the people who have messed up their lives the worst, even those who have fallen into the grossest selfishness and sin. And then he took one incredible additional step: he said he was going to die for precisely those kinds of people.

Jesus' radical acceptance of those who had harmed themselves, their families, and their neighbors was not based on some kind of cheap indulgence. In fact he said that harming other people is not just an awful offense against the neighbor; it is also a terrible affront against the Creator who created neighbors in the divine image. Therefore oppressors and sinners are God's enemies because they disrupt the harmony of God's good creation. But Jesus said God loves even these enemies so much that he would die for them. As God in the flesh, Jesus Christ said he would take all the evil of God's sinful enemies upon himself. Because he loved them, he would take on himself the punishment they deserved for their violence, oppression, and sin. At the cross, God himself suffered the agony of Roman crucifixion for the sake of sinful enemies. *That* is the foundation of Jesus' call to love our enemies. Jesus knew that the Creator of the galaxies loves his enemies enough to suffer incredible agony for them—*that* is why he taught his followers to love *their* enemies also.

But isn't that just utopian drivel? Don't we live in a violent, vicious

world where loving our enemies does not work? Didn't Jesus' life
end in failure at the cross?

That would be a proper conclusion except for one thing: Jesus
did not stay dead. On the third day, he was alive again. On Easter
morning the tomb was empty. By raising Jesus from the dead, God
proved that Jesus' way of loving his enemies was not naive utopian-
ism, but God's way to peace. By raising Jesus from the dead, God
proved the correctness of Jesus' teaching that God was busy restor-
ing the broken beauty of human society.

It is because I know that the Peacemaker from Nazareth rose
from the dead that I have hope today. It is because I know that the
Teacher of peace was God in the flesh that I dare to commit my
life to the long, costly struggle for nuclear disarmament.

I don't say that easily. I don't for a minute suppose that I can
persist in the long twenty-five-year struggle against nuclear holocaust
in my own strength. Let's not kid ourselves. Nuclear disarmament
will not happen in a year or two or three, even if—please God—we
can one day soon elect a President committed to nuclear disarmament
rather than nationalistic superiority. If nuclear disarmament comes
at all, if we succeed in avoiding nuclear holocaust, it will happen
only after long, exhausting decades of costly struggle.

Why than do _I_ hope to be able to walk that long and weary
road? Christians believe that the Risen Lord Jesus now lives in
those who open their lives to him. As Paul said, "It is no longer I
who live but Christ who lives in me." From personal experience, I
know that the Risen Jesus lives in me. I know that he calls me to
oppose nuclear madness—because creation is a divine gift to be
treasured, because every human life is sacred, because God loves
his enemies and calls on me to love my enemies. I cannot do that
in my own strength. But I don't have to, because Christ lives in me.

My friends, the task before us is awesome. The next two decades
will be the most dangerous in human history. But we can succeed.
We can rid the world of the monstrous evil of nuclear weapons. The
Creator of the galaxies is on the side of peace. In realistic political
terms, nuclear disarmament looks extremely difficult to achieve.
But it is not impossible. With God all things are possible. Let's
join him to make the planet safe for your children and mine.

I Didn't Know the Gun Was Loaded

MOST REVEREND L. T. MATTHIESEN
Roman Catholic Bishop, Diocese of Amarillo, Texas

Love your enemies. (Matt. 6:44)

Grace and peace be to you from the Lone Star State, from the high plains of Texas—where the buffalo roam no more; where a few deer and antelope still play, hiding from hunters in the thickets along the Canadian River; where much more than seldom are heard discouraging words about inflation, about the rapidly receding waters of the Olgalalla aquifer, and about the low price of wheat and cattle (though not of oil); and where those who know shudder to see the specter of monstrous mushroom clouds rising over Pantex, the final assembly point for all nuclear warheads manufactured in the United States. Located just fifteen miles from where I have lived for the past thirty-three years as priest, principal, editor, and now as Bishop, Pantex is often in my thoughts these days, thrust there by the troubled conscience of one of its employees, by the Pantex Six who scaled the outer security fence in a protest demonstration, and by the MX missile hearings—all intruding themselves on my heretofore largely untroubled world.

My world began in 1921 on a cotton farm in Central West Texas where my grandfather had settled after he left Germany in 1870 to seek a farm and a wife—and to escape the interminable wars of his day. In the words of my Aunt Hattie, he "did not like war."

My father too turned out to be something of a pacifist, though he seems readily to have acceded when at the age of twelve I suggested it would be nice if Santa Claus gave me a rifle for Christmas. The weapon of my dreams proved to be a .22-caliber single-shot Stevens. It was precious to me. I cleaned the barrel and oiled

[Delivered September 1981 at the Riverside Church, New York, N. Y.]

the stock frequently, and felt only a little less happy when Papa quietly talked about how guns can be used—and misused. He told about seeing a Texas Ranger along the Rio Grande shoot a Mexican in the back when the Mexican, who apparently could not speak English, turned in fear and ran after being accosted by the officer.

I had chance encounters with other guns through the years. Once, in a pickup, a rifle I was holding in my hands went off accidentally. The bullet sped within inches of a friend's head. I said, limply, "I didn't know the gun was loaded."

The last time I fired a gun was on a deer hunt. The deer I aimed at in the telescopic sights looked enormous, but close up it turned out to be little more than a fawn.

My last experience with a gun came as I stood helpless over the paralyzed body of a young man, the victim of an unthinking friend who had been showing off a pistol. The friend said, carelessly, "I didn't know the gun was loaded."

I know I will never own a gun again. I don't look at guns anymore through the eyes of a twelve-year-old.

After I released my public statement about the assembling of the neutron bomb at Pantex, a member of the staff of our church paper polled fifty students at West Texas State University at Canyon, thirty-five miles from Pantex. The majority of the students had never heard of Pantex, and those who had did not know exactly what it was for. They literally did not know that thermonuclear warheads capable of massive destruction are being loaded out there. In deference to the students, it should be noted that neither did the director of our Diocesan Office of Social Justice, though she made ample amends for that.

A former employee at Pantex wondered out loud why I had issued a statement against the neutron bomb. "After all," she observed, "the neutron bomb destroys buildings and tanks and things like that but does not hurt people." When someone said, "No, it's the other way around: the bomb destroys people, vaporizes and cremates them, but does not harm buildings and tanks with its radiation," her mouth fell open. She honestly did not know what was being loaded into the guns at Pantex. She just didn't know.

That, I submit, is our major problem: we don't know, and sadly, some of us would rather not know. We are still thinking in traditional terms—of self-defense, of armies meeting on battlefields far removed from civilian populations, of honor and glory. We simply do not know. I'm sure that is the situation because until very recently that is where I was in my own understanding.

I really paid little attention when the atomic bombs were dropped on Hiroshima and Nagasaki in 1945. I was grateful only that the war would soon be over and that my brother could come home. I did not realize at the time what the guns over Hiroshima and Nagasaki were loaded with.

Neither did Father George Zabelka, the Catholic chaplain who served as pastor to the airmen on Tinian Island, those flyers who manned the planes from which the atomic bombs were dropped. The Catholic community in Amarillo was in shock recently over the rape and killing of one nun on the eve of All Saints, 1981. But Father Zabelka and the Catholic pilot of the plane thought what they were doing was "necessary" when on August 9, 1945, they dropped on Nagasaki a bomb that destroyed *three entire orders of Catholic nuns*—along with forty thousand men, women, and children as well. But it is not just the atomic bombing that Father Zabelka recalls today with horror and remorse. He remembers also the thousands who were conventionally firebombed and napalmed in Tokyo, Dresden, Hamburg, Coventry, and Vietnam. Today he says: "I knew that civilians were being destroyed. Yet to the men who were doing it I never preached a single sermon against killing civilians. On Judgment Day I think I am going to need to seek more mercy than justice in this matter."

What of us? What of me? For thirty-three years I lived and continue to live at the very portals of Pantex, and for those thirty-three years I said nothing either as a priest or as Bishop—until a Catholic employee and his wife came to me with troubled consciences. They had begun to think that what he was doing at the plant was wrong.

Other events had preceded their coming. There had been a public hearing on the feasibility of locating the MX missile system to the west of Amarillo. Then there was the protest demonstration of the Pantex Six, the announcement about the neutron bomb, and an investigation into the feasibility of dumping radioactive waste in the Panhandle. I was finally moved to speak out. I had come to realize, with Martin Luther King, Jr., that the choice really is between nonviolence and nonexistence. Finally, I could no longer say, "I didn't know the gun was loaded."

I had come to agree with Father Zabelka that, in my church at least, "communion with Christ cannot be established on disobedience to his clearest teachings. Jesus authorized none of his followers to substitute violence for love—not me, not you, not the President, not the Pope, not anyone. Christ's teaching to love our enemies is not optional."

What followed the release of my statement was a revelation to me. The peace movement, I discovered, is very strong in the United States. The mail to my office is running over 95 percent in favor of nuclear disarmament. With the same and even more insistent demand coming from Central Europe, the time is here to evangelize the world —to deliver the good news that we can live without nuclear weapons, and that more and more people are ready and willing to do so.

When people are told the horror of the catastrophe being prepared for them by the industrial-military complex, they choose peace through disarmament. We simply must challenge the unholy alliance that prostitutes itself for short-term gain and spews forth its monstrous instruments of death.

In my town guns are for decorating the cabs of pickups. Guns are romanticized and relied on as if we were still living in the days of the old Wild West, when differences could be settled on Polk Street by single combatants confronting each other at high noon. Today it *is* high noon on Main Street, Planet Earth, but the characters in the broad-brimmed hats are not Clint Eastwood and Gary Cooper— they are those horrible dealers in death whose guns are loaded with noonday suns that vaporize and cremate and sow cancer. The guns *are* loaded. We need to know that, and we must say: no more. We threw off the slavery of Egypt, the slavery of Rome, the slavery of our own antebellum South. And we will throw off the slavery of the nuclear bomb. We will be slaves to fear no more.

In my town the community leaders shook their heads over my statement and said, "The Bishop is an idealist. We wish we could do what he urges, but we live in a real world and in this real world we must arm ourselves with nuclear weapons in order to defend our free way of life, our economy, and yes, even our churches."

I suggest that this is the greatest unreality, the greatest illusion of all. Pile the stocks of nuclear arms as high as you will, refine them as expertly as you wish, you cannot thereby deter others from doing the same. Indeed, you force them, in their delusion, to do so too. And speak not of stockpiles in country after country as a "safeguard"; such stockpiling only insures the final reality—a world at the point of no return, civilization being vaporized in the white heat of the final noonday sun.

I leave it to the scientists to tell the story in terms of destructive force, chain reactions out of control, the widening circle of radiation, the stripping away of the ozone layer. Indeed, I beg the scientists to tell the story to their colleagues and to all of us.

I leave it to the physicians to tell the story in terms of crushed bones and bleeding bodies, vaporization and cremation, skin melting away, leukemia and lingering death, altered genes, polluted streams and fields, shattered hospitals. Indeed I beg the physicians to tell the story to their colleagues and to all of us.

My task is to tell the story from the perspective of a man who believes in God, out of the conviction of a citizen whose nation boasts "In God We Trust," a searcher of the Scriptures that say, "Put up your sword, for those who live by the sword will die by the sword. Love your enemies. Do good to those who hate you."

And *you* must tell your story on the basis of whatever convinces you that the nuclear arms race is the ultimate madness, and that peace is possible because we yearn for it, we will work for it, and yes, we are willing to die for it.

Together we can overcome. Together we can compel the governments and the industrialists and the militarists to stop building nuclear bombs and to dismantle those that exist.

We have no alternative but to raise our voices, to speak out loudly, clearly, and continuously—until we achieve victory. If we do not do so, then let us pray that somewhere somehow a survivor will be left to speak in our name, to say of us: "They didn't know the gun was loaded."

It's a Sin to Build a Nuclear Weapon

WILLIAM SLOANE COFFIN, JR.
Senior Minister, The Riverside Church, New York, N.Y.

Early in the morning he [Jesus] came again to the temple; all the people came to him, and he sat down and taught them. The scribes and the Pharisees brought a woman who had been caught in adultery, and placing her in the midst they said to him, "Teacher, this woman has been caught in the act of adultery. Now in the law Moses commanded us to stone such. What do you say about her?" This they said to test him, that they might have some charge to bring against him. Jesus bent down and wrote with his finger on the ground. And as they continued to ask him, he stood up and said to them, "Let him who is without sin among you be the first to throw a stone at her." And once more he bent down and wrote with his finger on the ground. But when they heard it, they went away, one by one, beginning with the eldest, and Jesus was left alone with the woman standing before him. Jesus looked up and said to her, "Woman, where are they? Has no one condemned you?" She said, "No one, Lord." And Jesus said, "Neither do I condemn you; go, and do not sin again."

John 8:2–11

The nations have sunk in the pit which they made;
in the net which they hid has their own foot been caught.

Psalm 9:15

And to those words from the Ninth Psalm let us add these of Winston Churchill: "The Stone Age may return on the gleaming wings of science, and what might now shower immeasurable blessings on mankind may even bring about its total destruction. Beware, I say, time may be short."

Time *is* short. Only yesterday we worried that one part of the

[Delivered Sunday, November 22, 1981, in Amsterdam, Holland, at the World Council of Churches Hearings on Nuclear Weapons and Disarmament]

globe couldn't protect itself from another part; today it's the whole that can't protect itself from the parts. Only yesterday nations at war targeted one another; today the whole world lives on the target. Our world has become a constantly wired and rewired, ever-ready bomb, and every day we wake up could well be the day it goes off—by accident. Yet Americans and Soviets continue to build weapons like the Trident submarine we Americans launched ten days ago, a ship which in an hour can kill many times more human beings than the six million Jews killed during the six years of World War II. It makes common sense blush. We're like alcoholics who know that liquor is killing them, yet always have a good reason for taking just one more drink.

"The Stone Age may return on the gleaming wings of science." Always tragic, war has now become preposterous. It is ridiculous to talk of a "defense" budget, a "Defense" Department, when there is no defense; to talk of national security when every attempt to enhance security by accelerating the arms race has inexorably diminished it. Neither the United States nor the Soviet Union are superior one to another; rather, both sides are weak to the point of helplessness before the threat of a nuclear holocaust. To stay the return of the Stone Age we have to realize that nuclear war simply isn't war—it's suicide. Hence it is a matter not for statesmen and generals to plan but for citizens to prevent. As for those who talk of a limited nuclear war, they are like a person walking into an ammunition dump, lighting a match, and saying, "Don't worry, I'm just going to blow up a few mortar rounds."

But Christians have more to say, something quite simple: God alone has the authority to end life on this planet—but human beings have the power. Since this power is so clearly not authorized by any tenet of the faith, Christians have to say that it's a sin not only to use, but even to *build* a nuclear weapon. The building and owning of nuclear weapons must be in the sight of the Almighty an abomination comparable to the buying and owning of slaves. Therefore in repentence lies our hope, the hope that we can recognize the crisis before it is validated by disaster. Repentance would give us two great insights not available to the unrepentant, insights about self-righteousness and about fear.

The historian Herbert Butterfield once wrote: "In the kind of world that I see in history there is one sin that locks people up in all their other sins, and fastens men and nations more tightly than ever in their predicaments, namely the sin of *self-righteousness.*" Self-righteousness concentrates all attention on the sins of others. Self-righteousness fights evil as if evil were something that arose totally outside of oneself. We Americans tend to think the sins of the Soviets so heinous that—by the standard illogic of comparison—their wickedness confirms our goodness. We are like the exultant Pharisees who were prepared to stone to death the woman caught in adultery. Interestingly enough, Jesus does not dispute the sin, or even the sentence of death. He simply suggests that it would be questionable for a person worthy of the death sentence to condemn anyone else to death: "Let him who is without sin among you cast the first stone." Jesus takes a conspicuous example of wrongdoing and uses it not to nourish our cherished self-righteousness but rather to bring awareness of the sin common to all human beings, and of the need we all share for repentance.

Today Jesus would not be "soft on Communism"—or on capitalism. But I can hear him saying, "Let the nation without sin among you aim the first missile." Were we Americans truly to hear Jesus' words, we would see that even if we are not one in love with the Soviets at least we are one with them in sin—which is no mean bond, for it precludes the possibility of separation through judgment. Were we truly to hear Jesus' words, Soviet missiles would remind us of nothing so much as our own; Soviet threats to rebellious Poles would call to mind American threats to rebels in El Salvador; and Afghanistan would prompt us to remember Vietnam. Saved from self-righteousness by a vision of our common humanity and sin, might we not, like the Pharisees in the story, lay down our weapons?

"Ah yes," some will protest, "but the Pharisees had nothing to fear from the woman; she was disarmed." The objection is valid, but it makes the point: *fear* is what arms us, not disarms us.

For this reason deterrence is finally a disastrous policy. To induce fear is not the best but the worst possible way to avoid conflict. Here are the words of a farseeing diplomat: "Fear begets suspicion and distrust and evil imaginings of all sorts till each government feels that it would be criminal and the betrayal of its country not to take every precaution, while every government regards the precautions of every other government as evidence of hostile intent." Spoken by British Foreign Minister Sir Edward Grey in 1913, these words describe a similar double standard today: *they* arm and it's evil; *we* arm and it's necessary for national security.

Deterrence is a disaster because "deterrence is not a stationary but a degenerative state" (E. P. Thompson). The repressed violence backs up into each nation's politics, economics, ideology, and culture. Fear increases selfishness. Fear refines ever more hideous weapons. Fear enlarges the government's control over its population and client states. Without doubt, the renewed Cold War of the 1980s is reinforcing the ugliest features in both American and Soviet societies. And we must remember a psychological factor: expectation without action becomes boring, so psychologically we are always pushed to fulfill our expectations.

Self-righteousness and fear—these are the twin enemies pushing us ever closer to the return of the Stone Age, the twin masters whom we cannot serve if we are to serve God as well. That is why I like George Kennan's proposal for "an immediate across-the-board reduction by 50 percent of the nuclear arsenals now being maintained by the two superpowers." It makes the point that Enemy Number One is not the Soviet Union *or* the United States but the weapons themselves! Would that our government were prepared with such a proposal when U.S. and Soviet representatives meet in Geneva.

But let us at least rejoice that during his speech of last Wednesday President Reagan's tone was less polemical than heretofore, that he talked of parity, not superiority, and that he uncoupled arms control from Soviet good behavior. At the same time we must regret that he did not start the negotiations by taking action. The problem is not the stated willingness of both sides to negotiate; rather it is that neither side has demonstrated its readiness to disarm. How fine it would have been had President Reagan ordered suspension of work on the neutron bomb, or called home 200 of the American bombers he did not mention in his speech and whose importance will now become the subject of endless and childish dispute. How fine it would be if tomorrow, from Bonn, President Brezhnev were to order the dismantling of some SS-20s. Given the devastating firepower that would remain, neither nation would be "jeopardizing" its security by such withdrawal or dismantling, for let us never forget how totally false is the popular idea that nuclear deterrence deters only when it is precisely balanced at every level. (Whatever happened to the notion of sufficiency?)

It is also regrettable that negotiations are about to begin with the principal parties concerned not even present. After all, it was the marching of European feet that produced these negotiations. I hope they will not rest, these feet—joined shortly by more American and Russian feet too—will not rest until their peace-loving owners are properly represented in the negotiations, until every last nuclear device has been removed from European soil, nay, from the face of the earth. Said President Eisenhower: "I like to think that people want peace more than governments. In fact, I think they want it so badly that one of these days governments had better get out of the way and let them have it."

It's a sin to build a nuclear weapon. In repentance lies our hope, the hope that we will recognize the crisis before it is validated by disaster. Either we quickly end the arms race or the arms race will surely end the human race. Of one thing only can we be more certain—of God's far-reaching mercy. To us today, as to that sad and lonely figure of long ago, come similar words of assurance and admonition: "Neither do I condemn you; go and build nuclear weapons no more."

Why All This Strife About Peace?

JIMMY R. ALLEN
President, Radio and Television Commission,
Southern Baptist Convention

Blessed are the peacemakers, for they shall be called the children of God.

Matt. 5:9

Few issues draw more emotional fire than the effort to wage peace in a warring world. Nuclear war protests involve increasingly large crowds in demonstrations all over the world. Pulpits that have always given token attention to peace themes are beginning to sound the notes of that gospel melody once again. Political leaders whose war rhetoric and promises of more awesome weapons have swept them into power have begun to read the barometers of public opinion and temper their war talk with peace talk. The mass media, which portray so graphically the drama and heartbreak of war's destruction, are making the question of human survival a matter of daily conversation.

Yet peace efforts continue to draw emotional fire. Intense nationalists attack the peace movement, claiming that talk of peace is setting the U.S. up for a loss of national identity and national goals through conspiracies for world government. Military leaders warn of a fatal weakening of our national strength and an erosion of our freedom in the process. Voices in the business community charge that the peace movement is out to destroy the free enterprise system, that collective economies stand to win ground if we reject military solutions to international competition.

Feelings run deep when we talk of war and peace. The yearning

[Delivered in slightly revised form August 5, 1982, at the Southern Baptist Peace Convocation held in Louisville, Kentucky]

39

for peace has deep emotional roots. Yet the efforts for peace spark a conflagration of anxiety, anger, and accusation that makes peacemaking a perilous pursuit.

However we may view the use of force in a tangled and sinful world, no one seriously questions the fact that today we are in a position totally different from any that humankind has ever experienced before. We have lived with "the bomb" long enough to be desensitized to its danger.

I remember an oration I gave in a college speech competition on the atomic bomb. I described in dramatic terms the underground control centers that would someday be built, the chain reaction of destruction that is set loose by an atom bomb, the chilling threat that radiation fallout poses for all human existence. At that time only one nation held the secrets of the bomb. We looked with horror at the threat it posed and we dreaded the day when some other world power might gain access to its awesome possibilities.

Today fifteen or twenty nations have the capacity to start such a chain reaction of destruction. The two superpowers alone have enough explosive potential to kill everyone in the other's population from eight to eighteen times. Yet the horror factor has somehow diminished! We even talk with straight faces about "preemptive first strikes" and about tens of millions of casualties as "tolerable levels of destruction." All of humanity has reason to be alarmed at the blasé attitude with which we now treat the issue of nuclear holocaust.

We speak of feeling overwhelmed by the complexity of the issues involved in peacemaking. At the same time, however, we all contribute to the creation of an atmosphere that allows decision makers to choose either the nuclear option or peace with justice in our world.

Jesus gave us a description of happiness and fulfillment in the kingdom of God. Embedded in it is a base from which Christians can move in a determined way through all the strife and help to establish peace: "Blessed are the peacemakers, for they shall be called the children of God."

The first thing to be said about peacemaking is that it is not an optional course in the university of Christian experience—it is a divinely required responsibility. All through the prophetic visions of the Old Testament the ideal of peace is held out as God's ultimate goal for his people. When Jesus comes to establish the New Covenant, he comes as the Prince of Peace. The drive toward peace with justice is fueled by the revelation of God's intention for his children. We must be at the task because the Father is involved in it.

There is also a unique timeliness about it for the days immediately ahead. I am convinced there is a rhythm about the way God deals with humanity. He has built a rhythm into all of creation. The tides and seasons, the rise and fall of sensitivity to his presence in revelation and revival, the very breathing in and breathing out of all living things testifies to the rhythms of God.

I believe that there are also rhythms to God's moral agenda for a flawed and struggling humanity, caught in a world separated from his perfect fellowship by sin. Our limited understanding of God is further limited by the powerful presence of evil, which confuses us through its deep entrenchment in human relationships. God has to deal with us within this framework of our flawed nature and our limited understanding. Upon a humanity so situated he pours out his spirit through the presence of the Holy Spirit in the lives of his children. He works with us intensely to correct and guide as we are convicted and repentant. In our individual journeys he empowers our faltering first steps. As we grow he raises moral issues to our consciousness. The fact that early on we inadequately perceive them does not seal us off from his power. Later, as we are convicted of them, our continued experience of that power is determined by our willingness to deal with these issues. Rejecting his leadership concerning them cuts us off from the power. Confession and commitment restore the fellowship and the power.

That same power works also for the total spiritual family. In the earliest days of the Christian revelation, slavery was a morally repugnant practice. Yet the New Testament has no blanket condemnation of that social sin. The New Covenant does reveal the worth of every person as one for whom Christ died. It does establish the bond of fellowship between men and women both in God's creation and especially in God's re-created community. Yet the Holy Spirit is poured out on slave and slaveholder alike. There came a time in the unfolding of his truth, however, when the Father seemed to place on the conscience of all humanity the heinous nature of slavery. Slaveholding became a moral issue to be dealt with. God had blessed in

spite of it, but the day was coming when he would not do so. Finally
we were ready for that truth to be understood and applied. To reject
it would mean a rejection of God's will and purpose for us. The
ending of slavery was a painful learning experience, argued about,
fought over, violently reacted against. But that is what finally happened when, in the rhythm of God, the time came for it to be dealt
with—and it was.

Other issues have been similarly rhythmed into the agenda of
God's family. In the 1960s it was the right of all persons to be freed
of segregation and discrimination. That issue was most dramatically
demonstrated in the United States with our civil rights movement.
However, the same stirrings of conscience were moving throughout
the whole human family. No segment of God's creation could any
longer reject his revealed intention for every person to be valued
and freed as a matter of principle. Attitudes still have to be condi-
tioned, and we are far from dispelling all prejudice. Most of the
Christian family, however, has repented and recognized the standards
of God in the matter of civil and human rights. The Father uses
many means to accomplish his agenda, but when the time comes for
an issue to be raised and dealt with it is.

Slavery, human rights—these are simply two illustrations of the
rhythms of God. Now the issue for our decade and beyond seems
to be the issue of human survival. One senses the concern on every
hand. Cynics say it is all due to media hype. They point out that we
live in a blip culture in which each day's burning issues quickly give
way to tomorrow's headlines, events, or fads—because our attention
span is so short and the media's appetite so voracious. However,
there seems to be something deeper and more profound at work
here. In areas of the world less subject to the bombardment of media
images than our American society, the thoughtful are asking about
survival for humanity.

The issue of survival arises in connection with questions about
world hunger, human reproduction, and nuclear war. These questions are on the minds of people all over the world. They are not
raised just by Communist propagandists, restless European youth,
and "unrealistic" preachers. The issues are so basic, so persistent,
and so grounded in the revelation of God to humankind that it
seems as if the Father has rhythmed them into his moral priorities

for the human family. In short, peacemaking is God's agenda for his people. It is a divinely required responsibility.

Beyond that, peacemaking is a divinely provided privilege. Its joy is commensurate with its price. When I was citing the stress factors in peacemaking—the complexity, confusion, opposition, and emotion—it may have sounded as if Christians are being hounded into peacemaking as quarry slaves of conscience. That would be an incomplete picture.

True, peacemakers often become the target of animosity. Some of us have learned by personal involvement that the road we are called to take is indeed arduous. When I went to Iran on an unofficial fact-finding mission during the American hostage crisis, I rediscovered how scarring the vilification process can be. I was prepared to deal with the hostility and hatred of the Iranian students and of the Ayatollah Khomeini—both of whom I confronted in personal dialogue. What I wasn't quite prepared for was the ease with which my fellow believers back home could question motives, criticize judgments, and reject the role of intervention in a situation in which all official channels were closed.

The price of peacemaking can indeed be high. However, to see only the costs is to miss the heart of the matter. Jesus' Beatitude tells us that peacemaking is a privilege. It means we are in tune with what the Father is doing. Peacemaking is his activity. To the degree that we enter into that work, we enjoy the tremendous privilege of partnership.

This sense of privilege is constantly demonstrated in the joy of evangelism. What is the sharing of good news with a lost and alienated sinner if it is not peacemaking? Jesus came to Calvary to absorb all the hostilities and agonies of estrangement between God and humanity—to provide the bridge to peace with God. To enter into the sharing of that peace with another is one of the highest privileges of the Christian experience.

The same fervor and drive that moves us to be partners with God in evangelism should characterize our partnership with the Father in peacemaking and all other realms of his activity. There is joy in such harmony with the Father, in knowing oneself to be in tune with his leadership. It is a joy beyond description.

Peacemaking is not only a divinely required responsibility and a divinely provided privilege. It is also a divinely empowered enterprise. The work is his and he does it.

When we are so much like the Father in what we do that people can call us the children of God, we also experience the response of the Father in endowing our lives and actions with his power. God does not propel us toward disobedience. When we are doing his will, however, he joys in our partnership, and fuels us with the power of his presence. His Spirit guides us into all truth, and that is essential to being a peacemaker. The issues are so complex, and we must prayerfully examine them. But facts are available if we search for them. Some people assume that only the experts can know enough to pass judgment. This paralysis needs to be broken. An incredible amount of information is in print and available to those who inquire. The facts can be known. Christians, of all people, are called upon to love the Lord their God with all their minds. Let us then learn more and more about the issues so we can move forward in seeking to establish peace with justice in our world.

The Spirit also helps us when we pray. The promise in Romans 8 is that he will intercede with and for us when we "know not what to pray for as we ought." The prayer for peace should never be perfunctory. It is the fountain of hope for human survival.

The Spirit is at work encouraging us to bring order out of chaos, justice in an unjust world, and peace with protection for the rights of all men and women. The task indeed seems overwhelming. But the Spirit is at work to remind us that we serve the King of Kings. The whole world, the universe, is in his hand. He ultimately rules in the affairs of humankind. Whatever we can do now to help actualize a portion of that ultimate relationship will be blessed of the Father. He empowers the enterprise.

Peacemaking is God's doing. It is he who makes us partners with him in the task and privilege. I say this not to extol the operation but to encourage our moving ahead with it. Peace is not created simply by praising it. As Henlee Barnette reminds us, "Jesus does not say, 'Blessed is the peace praiser.' He says that it is the peacemaker who is blessed."

The God Who Stamps Out War

ROBERT McAFEE BROWN
Professor of Theology and Ethics, Pacific School of Religion

From end to end of the earth he stamps out war; he breaks the bow,
he snaps the spear and burns the shield in the fire.

Psalm 46:8-9 (NEB)

We've all had the experience: we are reading along in a familiar
piece of literature—a poem, a play, a passage of Scripture—and all
of a sudden something hits us in the text that we never noticed
before. Words that have previously slid off our tongues suddenly
choke in our throats or emerge with an unprecedented impact.

We read, for example, the Magnificat, Mary's Song at the beginning of Luke's Gospel. It starts out being what it always was—the
response of a dutiful, humble Jewish maiden who is properly obei-
sant when confronted by an angel and agrees, in gentle fashion, to
be the handmaiden of the Lord. And then, as for the first time, we
hear what this dutiful, humble Jewish maiden is actually saying:
God has "put down the mighty from their thrones, he has exalted
those of low degree, he has filled the hungry with good things, and
the rich he has sent empty away." This is Mary? The lady dressed in
blue? Why, she is sounding a call for social revolution! Why did we
never hear it that way before?

Much the same thing happens when we confront Psalm 46 as
though for the first time. It has rich associations for most of us as
the psalm that gives us courage, that reminds us of how all-encom-
passing is God's power. We recall Luther's stirring hymn "A Mighty
Fortress Is Our God," which is based on the first verse of the psalm.
We think of a God of strength and power who can sweep away every

---

[Delivered in slightly revised form February 28, 1982, at First Presbyterian
Church, Palo Alto, California]

impediment to the fulfillment of the divine will. Look out, world, Yahweh is on the march!

Then, with all that in mind, the rug is suddenly pulled out from under our elaborate theological construction. For what is this strong and mighty God doing? The God of the psalm is destroying not warriors, but the instruments of war—bows, spears, shields. The God of the psalm is stamping out not those rulers who have a propensity to wage war, but war itself. A rude shock, particularly to those who keep trying to fit the God of the Hebrew Scriptures into the mold of some kind of angry, thunderbolt-hurling deity. No— what emerges here is a God who breaks not bones, but the devices human beings use to break bones, a God who stamps out war itself.

The whole psalm deserves a fresh look. We can begin by reaffirming the well-known, underlying assurance that God *is* "our shelter and our refuge, a timely help in trouble" (v. 1). This is not only an introductory character reference, but a claim that is repeated, as a kind of chorus, on two further occasions: "The Lord of Hosts is with us, the God of Jacob is our high stronghold" (vv. 7, 11). All of which means, as the psalmist immediately goes on to affirm, that "we are not afraid" (v. 2). In the Revised Standard Version the claim and the exhortation are connected by a "therefore": God is our strength, *therefore* we will not fear.

That is the faith that has sustained the Jews through centuries of persecution, exile, and anti-Semitism (often at the hands of Christians). And that is the faith that has likewise sustained Christians in their own times of tribulation, whether under Nero, Hitler, or other dictators of our own day. There is a marvelous courage that these verses have both elicited and sustained, and nothing that can face us now or in the future is to be allowed to undo it. Back to square one. Here is a faith we can count on.

But then a tiny voice rises up in us and points out that while such faith was all very well for people in ancient times, or even in Luther's time, things are more complicated now. We no longer live in an age when "total disaster" might affect only a portion of the Mediterranean basin or even—at a later time—the whole of Europe. We now live in an age when every living creature on the face of the earth could disappear in a flash of fire and a mushroom cloud. And we are appalled at the scary prospect.

When such a mood strikes us, we need to look beyond the open-ing words of the psalm to those that immediately follow. Here we discover that the psalmist is not just talking about reassurance in the midst of local battles or regional disputes. When are we not to fear? "When the earth heaves and the mountains are hurled into the sea, when its waters seethe in tumult and the mountains quake . . ." (vv. 2–3). In another translation we are told not to fear "though the earth should change, though the mountains shake in the heart of the sea; though its waters roar and foam, though the mountains tremble with its tumult" (RSV). It goes without say-ing that the ancient psalmist was not trying to predict a nuclear holocaust, but it ought also to go without saying that the images describe remarkably well what we now know to be some of the phenomena that would characterize such an event. If this, for the psalmist, is a vision of what some apocalyptic act far off in the future might be like, it is also, for us, a description of what a specific human act in the immediate future might be like. Yet even in the face of such a possibility we are counseled not to fear: God is still "our shelter and refuge, a timely help in trouble"—even in such troubles as this.

We mustn't cheat on the text, however. The writer was surely *not* forseeing an event that demonic human ingenuity would bring to pass, but an event that would be encompassed within the purposes and action of God, almost (the images suggest) a kind of purging flood, a catastrophe that would render a new start possible. If there is one thing we are *not* entitled to do, however, we who live in the post-Hiroshima era—it is to suggest that any kind of man-made nuclear holocaust could have a beneficent outcome, or somehow be encompassed within the will of God. And that means that what-ever ultimate resources our faith provides may not be used to lull us into passivity or unconcern in the face of the threat of nuclear extinction. If we were to read only these first few verses of Psalm 46, that could conceivably be the outcome of our reflection. Fortu-nately, the psalm goes on and the verses that follow are the ones that suddenly hit us in a new way—and force us to think and act in new ways.

What is God doing in the face of all this trouble? "Nations are in tumult," the psalmist reports, "kingdoms are hurled down," and when God thunders, "the earth surges like the sea" (v. 6), ór, as another translation puts it, "the earth melts" (RSV).

The earth melts? What kind of a God is this? Will God bring about the ultimate devastation? What is God doing anyway?

The psalmist has anticipated our question: "Come and see what the Lord has done," the writer invites us, "the devastation he has brought upon the earth" (v. 8)—which still sounds scary and destructive. But what *is* the "devastation"? Clearly, it is the devastation to human plans and national ambitions. No wonder "nations are in tumult and kingdoms are hurled down," for *this* is the devastation that God brings. Listen: "From end to end of the earth he stamps out war; he breaks the bow, he snaps the spear and burns the shield in the fire." Devastation indeed to nations who want more instruments of war; devastation indeed to those who would like to stockpile more bows, spears, and shields.

Here is truly an unexpected turn of events. We are hearing about a powerful God, about tumult on the earth, about armies pitted against armies, and we have every reason to expect that God will align the divine power behind one side or the other to see to it that the good guys win.

But no. Apparently nobody is to win—or lose—because, amazingly, the very instruments of war are themselves to be destroyed. Let us be quite clear about what this means. We may be tempted lightly to dismiss bows, spears, and shields as outmoded, as having little military significance for us, as being peripheral to our world of warfare. And indeed they are. But at the time of the psalmist those weapons were the central instruments of warfare. Today the counterpart of a bow would be an M1 rifle; the counterpart of a spear, the Trident missile; and the counterpart of a shield, the policy of nuclear deterrence. God, the psalmist's original hearers would have learned, is not concerned just to destroy outmoded weapons, to make only a token gesture in the direction of peace. No, the divine disarmament program here described aimed at what today we call the "biggies," the really destructive instruments, those on the basis of which nations make foreign policy, seek to defend themselves, and initiate invasions when they think they can get away with it.

How does God propose to "stamp out war"? Clearly, in this

account, by getting rid of the means for making war—a divine disarmament plan.

Let us not claim that the psalmist thus puts a seal of divine approval on the nuclear freeze movement, or that we have here a detailed blueprint for efforts to "reverse the arms race." But it would be pretty hard to avoid the implication that if we take Psalm 46 seriously we will also have to take seriously a nuclear freeze— and, beyond that, all kinds of proposals not simply for limiting the use of nuclear weapons (and ultimately all weapons) but for getting rid of them altogether. Breaking, snapping, burning are the verbs used to describe what should be done to the major weapons of warfare. That is certainly the divine intention, and the burden of proof lies on those who say otherwise.

If the destruction of arsenals is the divine intention, it should be the human intention as well. When the psalmist shifts from talking about God to talking about us, we may not get a master blueprint for explicit action, but implicitly we get a whole closet full. Explicitly, we are simply told, "Let be then; learn that I am God . . ." (v. 10), or in another translation, "Be still, and know that I am God" (RSV). Whatever those generalized directions mean, they clearly counsel letting go of aggressive policies that lead to further weapons buildup, forsaking attempts to "seize the initiative" against our so-called "enemies." "*Arrêtez!*" the French version says— "*Stop* all this nonsense." And one commentator points out that the commandment to "Be still" means very explicitly "Lay down your arms."

Implicitly, when we couple the injunction "Let be" with the affirmation following it, "learn that I am God," we are being reminded that our temptation is always to let something other than God be our god—in this case the weapons of war. Weapons are our god when we place our trust in them. And the whole movement of the psalm is designed to counter that: It is *God* who is "our refuge and strength." It is *God* who is "a timely help in trouble." It is "the Lord of Hosts" who is with us, "the God of Jacob" who is "our high stronghold."

The emphasis is not unique to the psalmist. We find it time and again in the Bible. Isaiah counsels Israel: "Woe to those who go down to Egypt for help and rely on horses, who trust in chariots

because they are many and in horsemen because they are very
strong, but do not look to the Holy One of Israel or consider the
Lord" (Isa. 31:1). Here it is chariots and horses, the basic instruments of invasion, that are not to be trusted—any more than tanks
or aerial assault forces are to be trusted today.

Psalm 46 moves in another direction as well. Those who claim
to be children of such a God, who claim to worship such a God,
who claim to be followers of such a God, have a clear mandate
placed on them: they may not act in ways that are contrary to the
will of this God. If God seeks to stamp out war, so must God's
children. If God seeks to break the bows, shatter the spears, and
burn the shields, so must God's children. Indeed, we can go so
far as to say that one way *God* seeks to stamp out war is through
the enlistment of *our* action to help bring about that end.

This does not provide us with the details of a foreign policy.
It does not furnish easy answers to the question, "What about the
Russians?" It does not tell us to be merely passive in the face of
evil. But it does insist that as we seek for the foundations of a
foreign policy, for a way of dealing with the Soviet Union, and for
an appropriate posture in the face of evil, the words of this psalm
must be our charter.

It is hard to see how we can claim to be believers in the Bible,
or more properly in the God of the Bible, and still urge the further
manufacture of nuclear weapons. It is hard to see how anyone can
take this psalm seriously without a renewed commitment to arms
reduction and ultimately arms elimination. It is hard to see how
we can honor this part of the Biblical message without developing
a whole new set of priorities about how we are to use our resources.
If we were to cut back, and then cease, the production of weapons,
that would release billions of dollars for creative projects—stamping
out world hunger and providing shelter, education, and health facili-
ties for the members of the human family who are denied such
things.

A risk? Of course a risk—but surely less of a risk than increasing
the production of weapons that can destroy us all. An act of faith?
Of course an act of faith—just as relying on weapons is an act of
faith, though faith in a different "god." The choice the psalmist
puts before us is clear: in disavowing faith in weapons, we are

asked to place our faith elsewhere. And the psalmist's directions are even clearer: we too are to stamp out war, break the bow, snap the spear, and burn the shield in the fire. Why? Because "the Lord of Hosts is with us, the God of Jacob is our high stronghold."

The Rainbow

KRISTER STENDAHL
Andrew W. Mellon Professor of Divinity, Harvard University

> When I bring clouds over the earth and the bow is seen in the clouds,
> I will remember my covenant which is between me and you and
> every living creature of all flesh; and the waters shall never again
> become a flood to destroy all flesh.
>
> Gen. 9:14–15

"Never again" would chaos and total destruction engulf the
earth. Never again would God despair of the creation.

God's will is clear. So clear that this covenant—the rainbow
covenant with all life on earth—is the only unconditional covenant
in the Bible. It does not say: ". . . provided that you behave." In
the bold language of the Bible, the rainbow will remind God of that
promise whenever God is tempted to despair of the beloved yet
troublesome experiment of humanity and the world.

God's will is clear. But what about us? The ancient teller of the
Noah story could not fathom that one day it would be possible
for human beings utterly to destroy the earth. Who could ever
have imagined it? But fear, greed, and technology have now created
just such a possibility by lethal chain reaction. There has been this
quantum jump: nuclear weapons are *not* just bigger guns. Today
God's unconditional rainbow covenant is threatened—by us!

And "us" spells the U.S. first, for we are the only nation that has
used such weapons. We did cross the barrier; we did take the quantum step. The world is aware of that. It adds to much fear that
someone did.

If they had said to me when I was a child, "Don't litter—you

[Delivered Sunday, May 16, 1982, on the steps of the town hall in Sudbury,
Massachusetts, at the Rainbow Covenant Celebration sponsored by the Sudbury Interfaith Committee Against Nuclear War]

52

may pollute the ocean; don't burn that—you may pollute the atmosphere," I would have considered it a joke. But now we know.
Imagine—irreversible pollution of our world. We know what a quantum jump in destructive power is.

We live in a world that overwhelms our sense of responsibility.
It is all too big, too much, and—as we say—too complicated. We
cannot take it all in. It is too threatening. It produces moral numb-
ness. We are tempted to opt out—in order to protect our sanity.
And so we tend to our private worlds, our suburban beauty with
white houses and glorious dogwood.

We do not want to give in to the temptation, the temptation to
become cynical. But we know: the cloud hangs over us—without a
rainbow.

There is a way—what Paul called the "more excellent way." That
is the way of sharing. Sharing also our fears. We are too weak and
too scared to be conscious of our fears all the time. So let us take
turns.

The rainbow has the full spectrum from cool colors to hot colors.
We can serve one another by taking turns thinking about the unthinkable. So, perhaps only so, can the crushing truth be kept
before us. So, perhaps only so, can we retain our sanity in an
insane world. So, perhaps only so, can we enliven and support one
another. That is *our* rainbow covenant, in sharing and in truth-
telling, in urgency and in tenacious patience.

The dove with the olive leaf—the symbol of peace—actually
comes from this same story in the Bible. The story has its roots in
ancient epics from Mesopotamia, the land Between the Rivers. Noah
sent out the dove three times in hope. The first time it came back,
for it found no ground; there were no signs of hope. The second
time, "the dove came back to him in the evening, and lo and behold,
in her mouth a freshly plucked olive leaf," the living sign of hope.
The third time, "she did not return to him anymore."

And then came the rainbow—with its full spectrum.

Gifts of Fire

JOAN CHITTISTER, OSB
Prioress, Benedictine Sisters of Erie, Pennsylvania
Past President, Leadership Conference of World Religious

When the day of Pentecost came it found them gathered in one place. Suddenly from up in the sky there came a noise like a strong, driving wind which was heard all through the house where they were seated. Tongues of fire appeared, which parted and came to rest on each of them. All were filled with the Holy Spirit.

Acts 2:1–4 (NAB)

There is a story told among Hasidic Jews that I think is important for Christians, important for Pentecost. This story is about a wise old rabbi whose insights were so clear, whose teachings so profound, that not only his own congregation but the rabbis in congregations of villages beyond the mountains looked to him for leadership. One day the wise old rabbi suddenly died. The young rabbis prayed sincerely that they might receive an infusion of his kind of spirit and, sure enough, one night the old master appeared to one of them during sleep. The young rabbi said, "Master, it's good that you've returned. Our people look to us for answers to the great questions of life and we do not know all the answers. Tell us, Master: on the other side, of what account are the sins of youth?" The old man replied: "The sins of youth? Why, on the other side the sins of youth are of no account whatsoever." And the young rabbi said, "The sins of youth are of no account whatsoever? Then what has it all been about? What *is* punishable on the other side?" And the old man answered: "That sin which is punishable on the other side with continual and unending severity is the sin of false piety."

[Delivered on Pentecost Sunday, May 30, 1982, in slightly revised form at the Pentecost Peace Witness of the Leadership Conference of Women Religious, held in Lafayette Park across from the White House in Washington, D. C.]

With the Hasidim, I submit that true fear of God demands that we know what piety is proper for our times.

It's easy for us to pray for the gifts of the Holy Spirit—if what prompts us is the love of praying and not the gifts themselves. But if we've come here today because we're intent on Pentecost and not simply on praying, then I beg of you: Beware. Because the gifts of the Holy Spirit are not for getting and keeping, but for giving and doing. They are not meant simply to condition and console. Wisdom, understanding, fortitude, counsel—such gifts of the Holy Spirit are important; the revelation, the insights, the endurance, and the direction they bring are certainly necessary. But our own consolation is not what Pentecost is all about. The flaming gifts of the Holy Spirit do not simply console; they commit, they compel, they cost, they cry out for creative change.

"Rabbi," the disciples demanded, "we pray, we fast, we read the Scriptures. Why then has the Messiah not come?" And the rabbi replied: "Wherefore has the son of Jesse not come, neither yesterday nor today? The Messiah does not come today because today we are no different than we were yesterday."

From this moment on, for us, that can never be true again. Tomorrow you and I will be different. Perhaps we will not be better, but we must definitely be different—because we have come today to pray the presence of Pentecost into our own lives. We have come together at this moment seeking the gifts of piety, knowledge, and fear of our God.

Do not be misled. We have not come here to pray for pietism; we have come to pray for *piety*. We have not come here to pray for the grace to practice private devotion; we have come to pray for dedication to the public, dutiful service of God. To pray for piety is to pray for the gifts of leadership and courage, strength and risk, gifts of which the Book of Wisdom speaks when it praises "those pious ones, your ancestors" who have gone before us: Moses and Aaron; Joshua and Caleb; Samuel and Solomon—leaders, judges, prophets, risk-takers all. We have come to pray for the piety to which Jesus called the Pharisees over and over again.

There are those who say that on Pentecost religious should be in their convents, not here in Washington, D. C. There are those who say that religious should mind their prayers, not the morality of politics. There are those who say that religious should concentrate on acts of mercy and forget the obstacles to justice. So domesticated has our piety become that people think it unreligious for religious to call the conscience of the king. Tell that to Jeremiah and Daniel, to Deborah and Judith. We have come to pray not for pietism but for piety.

We have come also to pray for *knowledge*—not for technical specialization but for a burning vision of the integrity between the sacred and the secular, the present and the eternal. And we have never needed knowledge more. In 1945, with the detonation of the atomic bomb, you and I witnessed one of the great watersheds of human history. A whole new age began, an age as distinct from the age that preceded it as the modern age is distinct from the Middle Ages, or the Middle Ages from antiquity.

Thirty-seven Pentecosts ago the old rules of war became obsolete, the old theologies of war became amusing, the old methods of war became meaningless—because what nuclear weapons seek to preserve they can only destroy. What we value must be preserved and defended some other way, or not at all. And until we find that other way we will have to abide "defenses" that undermine domestic development without promoting peace. Defense takes from the poor: we have reduced social welfare funding by $57 billion in two years. Defense terrorizes the vulnerable: we have increased our military spending by $33 billion in one year. Defense threatens our very existence: it is based not on national security, but on national suicide and national insolvency. Defense has replaced the welfare state with the military state: we have diverted our national wealth and resources away from housing, away from the assault on poverty, away from research, away from the arts. We have chosen to be Sparta rather than Athens.

Victor Frankl, the Jewish psychiatrist and survivor of German concentration camps, says that in time of crisis people do one of three things: they deny it ("It's not that bad." "It will never happen."); or they despair ("There is nothing anyone can do; we must simply live through it and pray."); or, they commit themselves to the asking of critical questions. Perhaps you and I, being who we are, cannot really do much, but we can at least give the gift of Christian discomfort. By knowing enough to say no, we can make it impossible for anyone to make war easily. And we can give others the knowledge they need to do the same. So we pray not only for piety but also for knowledge.

We are praying, too, for a holy *fear of God*. We have learned to fear the mysterious, powerful, unknown Other, but we have forgotten to fear the just God who made *them* as well as *us*. We have learned to fear other people and the possibilities of human trust, but we have forgotten to fear the insidious effects of Christian schizophrenia as we talk of peace and prepare for nuclear annihilation. We have learned to fear the enemy, but we have forgotten to fear ourselves, we who created the first atomic bomb, produced the first hydrogen bomb, deployed the first armed ICBMs, and first invented multiple warheads.

We have not feared to seek and develop the weapons of war, but we have feared to wage peace with the same intensity. In 1980 the annual budget for the Commission on Arms Control and Disarmament was less than half of what the Department of Defense spends on military bands. To those who ask: "Isn't deterrence essential?" I say: "Isn't once enough!"

Yes, we will be different tomorrow if we pray seriously—for piety, for knowledge, and for fear of our God. We will be different, but not necessarily better. For though the gifts of the Holy Spirit can be inspiriting, they can be sinned against too. The sin against piety is to choose private devotion rather than our public duties to creation. The sin against knowledge is to know that something must be done but then do nothing at all. The sin against the fear of God is to be silent in a world that is both materially and morally underdeveloped.

Pentecost can mean power. For us it can mean the power not to give over our own power to people who want to name our enemies. No, we must stand instead like Esther, who went to the king though she was not called; like Judith, who put herself between the besieging army and her defenseless people because any other defense would have been totally destructive. We must *not* stand like Samson, who combined not strength and vision but power and blindness, a tragic combination. Yes, Samson brought down the temple upon his enemies, but in so doing he destroyed himself as well. As a nation our strength can hardly be impaired, but our vision can be lost. We must realize that there is nothing more dangerous than a frustrated, frightened giant who fears the wrong things.

Remember, too, that if today we have asked for gifts, the gifts are also ours to give: to speak the truth in public; to say no and teach others to say no; to distinguish piety from patriotism, knowledge from nationalism, and fear of God from the fear of force; to renew our own lives; to renew a universal concern for others; and to renew the face of the earth.

What can we do? We can learn in our time from the pieties of the past. An ancient monastic story tells of a religious who wanted to be holy and who said to her spiritual guide: "According as I am able, I keep my little rule; I do my little fast, my prayer, my meditation, my contemplative silence, and according as I am able I strive to cleanse my heart from evil thoughts. Now, holy one, what more should I do?" The elder rose up, stretched her hands all the way to heaven, and her fingers became like ten lamps of fire. And the holy one said, "If you want to be holy, why not be totally changed into fire?"

What more can *we* do? We can keep our little fasts, sign our little cards, wear our little buttons, say our prayers, and according as we are able cleanse our hearts of evil thoughts. But more than that, we too can arm! We can arm ourselves with piety, with knowledge, and with the fear of our God. Whether we are received at those White House gates or not, as holy people of our time we can exert a powerful feminine influence in a world reeling from machomania. We can, if we want, if we truly want, if we *deeply* want—at this new Pentecost point we can be turned, you and I, courageously, consumingly, completely, into new Pentecost fire. The question is addressed to every one of us, to every convent, every church, every Christian everywhere: for God's sake, why not be totally changed into fire?

Spiritual Weapons for Waging Peace

VERNON C. GROUNDS
President Emeritus, Conservative Baptist Seminary,
Denver, Colorado

> I urge, then, first of all, that requests, prayers, intercession and thanksgiving be made for everyone—for kings and all those in authority, that we may live peaceful and quiet lives in all godliness and holiness. This is good, and pleases God our Saviour, who wants all men to be saved and to come to a knowledge of the truth.
>
> 1 Tim. 2:1–4 (NIV)

On this Memorial Day weekend we are privileged to be worshipping God in peace and quietness, freedom and security. Once our worship is ended, most of us will be going back to comfortable homes where we will have more than enough to eat. Like most Americans, we are probably struggling with three serious problems: One, where do I park my car? Two, who's going to win the game? Three, how do I lose weight? Yes, those are pressing problems indeed! As we worship here today, we are thankfully and solemnly honoring the memory of those men and women who died in defense of the liberty, equality, and democracy that we take for granted. And we hope that God will somehow make us aware of our privileges and grateful for what we have as citizens of this unquestionably great republic.

As we meet here for worship in quietness and peace, we realize that people all around the earth—many of them children—are living in tumult, fear, and misery. Many are our brothers and sisters in Jesus Christ. We realize that these people have the same feelings and needs, hopes and dreams that we have. But they are living in

[Delivered May 30, 1982, at Bear Creek Evangelical Church, Denver, Colorado]

59

countries ruled by dictators. They are living in countries without
adequate food and clothing and medicine. They are living in countries where war is raging. So I feel constrained today to lay a burden
concerning them on all our hearts.

I can't blame you for reacting negatively to the thought of an
added burden. You may be carrying enough burdens already, burdens
of personal worry, grief, and tension. As Christians, trying to be
obedient disciples and conscientious citizens we also carry a heavy
burden of spiritual and moral concerns. We are concerned about
corruption on every level of our society—reaching even into the
highest echelons of government. We are concerned about all those
evils that destroy, demean, and diminish human life—abortion,
cancer-causing tobacco, alcoholism, drunken driving, drug addiction,
pornography, family breakdown, sexual promiscuity, environmental
pollution, crime, injustice, racism. Well, that's a heavy burden of
concern.

But in addition to all these other concerns we need to become
concerned about the possibility of war. What will nuclear war be
like? We are sitting home casually having breakfast; there's a flash,
there's a blast, and we are engulfed in a fireball which reduces us
to cinders. We are walking with our family in the park; there's a
flash, there's a blast, and when we regain consciousness, we try
to drag our dying bodies towards the charred remnants of our
children. We're standing on Lookout Mountain with some friends
from the East, pointing with pride to the burgeoning Denver skyline;
there's a flash, there's a blast, and the city is gone like an egg
crushed under a steamroller. That's what we face if nuclear war
occurs, and that's why on this special day when we solemnly honor
those who died in our nation's past wars, I have prayerfully decided
to focus our attention on what the word of God has to say about
Christian responsibility for peacemaking and peacekeeping.

First, we must remind ourselves that our God, the God of our
Lord Jesus Christ, is the God of peace. Because we tend to overlook
this essential attribute of the divine character, let us consider what
Scripture discloses concerning God as the God of peace. In the
New Testament there are at least seven references to this facet of
God's nature. In Romans 16:20, for example, Paul assures us that
"the God of peace will soon crush Satan under your feet." Second

Corinthians 13:11 is another text that highlights peace as a divine attribute: "Finally brethren, farewell. Mend your ways. . . . Live in peace, and the God of love and peace will be with you." Still another text, the great doxology in Hebrews 13:20, refers to "the God of peace who brought again from the dead our Lord Jesus Christ."

All these texts proclaim that God is the God of peace. God is never at war with himself. The members of the Trinity don't engage in strife and quarreling. That would be unthinkable. No, God is the God of peace, and therefore he wills peace and he wants peace among the nations on our planet.

Second, we must remind ourselves—and it's appropriate on this Memorial Day weekend to do so—that if there is war on earth we can't blame God for it. By no means! In 1 Corinthians 14:33 Paul declares: "God is not the God of confusion. He is the God of peace." So if war comes, we human beings are to blame. We are responsible. We sinfully choose violence and bloodshed and death instead of harmony and brotherhood and life.

The apostle James tells us in a hard-hitting letter to some first-century Christians who had been scattered abroad by persecution that if there is strife, if there is war, if there is violence, you can't blame God. God doesn't will it. Human wickedness causes war. Though James is not a sociologist, he gives us a profound analysis of why history is a terrible record of marching armies and bloody battles: "What causes wars, and what causes fightings among you? Is it not your passions that are at war in your members? You desire and do not have; so you kill. And you covet and cannot obtain; so you fight and wage war" (James 4:1-2). Ruthless ambition, greed for land and gold and power, fierce hatred and cruel envy—these are the root causes of war: not the will of God, but the wickedness of man.

Human sin has brought on and still brings on the terrible scourge of war. How can I denounce that scourge enough? It is war that destroys the world's resources while people suffer, starve, sicken, shiver, and perish. It is war that destroys millions upon millions of human beings, each of them created in the image of God and ticketed with the price tag of Calvary. Think of war's indescribable agony and mutilation, terror and heartache. Think of how it breeds pestilence, disease, and famine. Think of how it sows the seeds of suspicion

and revenge in the field of international relations. As Civil War
general William Tecumseh Sherman put it, "War is hell." You
don't need to endorse his language or agree with his theology in
order to admit that he was right. War is a devilish business that
originates in the depths of satanic depravity.

Third, we must remind ourselves today that the God of peace,
who wills peace, calls upon you and me as disciples of Jesus Christ
to be peacemakers. All of us are familiar with the beatitude recorded
in the Sermon on the Mount: "Blessed are the peacemakers" (Matt.
5:9). But perhaps we are not as familiar with James 3:18: "The
harvest of righteousness is sown in peace by those who make peace."
However heroic and patriotic soldiers and sailors may be, war
requires ghastly violence. It compels people to perform acts that,
performed in civilian life, would horrify their hearts and consciences.
War produces every kind of unrighteousness; it breeds a harvest of
evil. Peace, according to James, produces a harvest of righteousness.
It is like a garden in which peacemakers sow acts of compassion,
forgiveness, and reconciliation; and the fruit of those peaceful acts
is righteousness.

So peace is the prerequisite for the establishment of God's
righteousness in the earth. If we are to have righteousness, we must
have peace. It's as simple as that.

The God of peace therefore summons us, as disciples of Jesus
Christ, to be peacemakers in our marriages, our homes, our friend-
ships, our neighborhoods, our churches, our places of business and
work, our country, and our world. The challenge is well put in the
words of Francis of Assisi: "Lord, make me an instrument of thy
peace. Where there is hatred, let me sow love; where there is injury,
pardon; where there is doubt, faith; where there is despair, hope;
where there is darkness, light; where there is sadness, joy." Oh, let
us offer that prayer sincerely: "Lord, make me an instrument of your
peace. Help me be a peacemaker who in peace sows the fruits of
righteousness."

Do we understand, though, that it's impossible to function as an
agent of reconciliation unless we have first been reconciled to God
by faith in the atoning death of Jesus Christ? Do we understand
that it's impossible to be a peacemaker unless we have first entered
into God's peace by coming to the cross and claiming pardon

through the sacrifice of our Lord Jesus Christ? Only when we have peace with God, his very peace in our own hearts, only then—and not before then—can we become peacemakers.

There's one other thing which we must not forget this Memorial Day weekend: God has put at our disposal effective weapons for waging peace. I know there is a fatalistic mood abroad these days. Some of us, misinterpreting prophecy, are convinced that we live in the end times and that we therefore cannot hope for peace. But prophecy is not fatalism. God *has* put at our disposal effective weapons for the waging of peace. If we grasp this fact, we will begin in faith to challenge the fatalistic mindset that sees nothing ahead but the horror of nuclear holocaust. In 2 Corinthians 10:3–5 Paul refers to these weapons: "For though we live in the world, we do not wage war as the world does. The weapons we fight with are not the weapons of the world. On the contrary, they have divine power to demolish strongholds. We demolish arguments and every pretension that sets itself up against the knowledge of God, and we take captive every thought to make it obedient to Christ." Do we really grasp the meaning of that passage? At our disposal we have weapons which, even at the end of the twentieth century, can bring to pass the purpose of God for the prevention of war and the preservation of peace. I believe with all my heart that you and I, as instruments of God's peace, can use these spiritual weapons and win the victory over the warmongering powers of evil.

And the mightiest weapon in that spiritual armament is prayer. I make that assertion on the basis of 1 Timothy 2:1–4: "I urge, then, first of all, that requests, prayers, intercession and thanksgiving be made for everyone—for kings and all those in authority, that we may live peaceful and quiet lives in all godliness and holiness. This is good, and pleases God our Saviour, who wants all men to be saved and to come to a knowledge of the truth." This is surely one of the great New Testament pronouncements on the purpose and effectiveness of prayer. We are urged to pray in order that, cooperating with God, we may establish a society of peace and quietness, a society within which the gospel can be freely proclaimed and people come to know Jesus Christ as Savior. What could be plainer?

Do you and I want quietness instead of turmoil? Then we must pray. Do we want godliness instead of immorality? Then we must pray. Do we want peace instead of war? Then we must pray. Do we want integrity instead of untruthfulness? Then we must pray.

Prayer is a weapon infinitely more powerful than all the guns and bayonets, tanks and planes, battleships and bombs of all the nations in all the world. I'm not minimizing the awesome decisions that officials in positions of governmental responsibility must make. I'm not minimizing the difficulties of preventing war. I'm simply affirming the conviction that there are no imaginable limits to the effectiveness of prayer. If we as God's people take even five minutes a day to follow the directive given to Timothy, God may be pleased to bestow peace in our time.

You and I have experienced something of God's peace in our own hearts. Let us, then, take more seriously than ever these words of Saint Francis, "Lord, make me an instrument of your peace." Let's give ourselves daily to a ministry of fervent intercession so that the will of God—the God of peace—may be done in our lives and on his earth.

The Bus

JOHN VANNORSDALL
Chaplain, Yale University

I am the good shepherd. The good shepherd lays down his life for
the sheep. He who is a hireling and not a shepherd, whose own the
sheep are not, sees the wolf coming and leaves the sheep and flees;
and the wolf snatches them and scatters them. He flees because he is
a hireling and cares nothing for the sheep. I am the good shepherd; I
know my own and my own know me, as the Father knows me and I
know the Father; and I lay down my life for the sheep. And I have
other sheep, that are not of this fold; I must bring them also, and
they will heed my voice. So there shall be one flock, one shepherd.

John 10:11–16

When I came out of the train station, I could see a bus approach-
ing, so I joined the crowd at the bus stop for a ride to the Green.
The driver opened the door and said something, but only the
people at the head of the line could hear what she said. By the
time I was close enough to drop my coins into the fare box, the
problem had become known to everyone: two young boys who
needed transfers had already dropped their money through the slot
before they discovered that the driver had no transfers. I gathered
from the conversation that the driver had no way of getting their
money out of the box again, and that one of the two boys had no
money left for boarding the next bus that would take him to his
destination.

It was at this point that some of the passengers got involved. One
observed to the driver: "There's a bus pulling up behind us"—
which prompted the driver's suggestion: "You fellows get on the
bus behind me and just tell them you've already paid."

[Delivered May 2, 1982, in Battell Chapel, Yale University, at a time when
the British invasion of the Falkland/Malvina Islands held by Argentine troops
seemed imminent]

65

"That driver ain't gonna believe those boys," objected another passenger. There was a murmur of agreement.

Our driver looked around at us helplessly as though to say, "Now you folks know I'm not supposed to leave this bus." But there was something in the face of the heavyset lady across from me, and of the man with the lunch pail, which seemed to convey: "It's all right, lady; we'll take care of the bus."

So our driver got off, walked quickly to the trailing bus, got some transfers, and returned and gave them to the two boys—who seemed relieved. Off we went with the usual roar while the lady sitting next to me shouted across the aisle, "She's new, but she's gonna do all right."

Two things are important about this episode. The first is that the passengers about me that day were very knowledgeable about buses. They knew the importance of a transfer, that the driver was unable to get money out of the box, and that she was reluctant to leave her bus. They knew, too, that the driver behind wouldn't believe the boys, and that our driver was new. In fact, I was the least knowledgeable passenger on board—a full two blocks beyond my stop before someone showed me how to push the signal button for getting off.

Now, it's all right that I'm not knowledgeable about buses—because I know some other things, and so do you. We are all knowledgeable about some things. Yale is a great knowledge factory. *Veritas*—truth—is our motto, but knowledge is our game. The two are not the same.

Knowledge is how to get a bus to stop; it's learning to describe the forces that powered the Westward movement in the United States; it's the capacity to observe, analyze, generalize, and test. To be knowledgeable is to have mastered a variety of processes, fingering, and irregular verbs. Knowledge is the capacity to recognize sounds and patterns, to distinguish ends from means, to remember what *has been*—for the purpose of either repeating or avoiding it, or to predict on the basis of what has been what *might be*.

Knowledge is ubiquitous. It facilitates a bus ride, and it fills the seas and the air of the South Atlantic with ships and planes. But a jump jet is knowledge, not truth.

Only fools spurn knowledge. Religious people cherish it. It is important to us that God *knows* us. The promise of today's text makes a difference: "I am the good shepherd; I know my own, and my own know me." "O God, thou knowest my folly; the wrongs I have done are not hidden from thee," wrote the psalmist. "O Lord, thou hast searched me and known me! Thou knowest when I sit down and when I rise up; thou discernest my thoughts from afar. . . . If I take the wings of the morning and dwell in the uttermost parts of the sea, even there thy hand shall lead me, and thy right hand shall hold me."

These words have been rehearsed in so many prisons, in distant airports, in trains and buses—by people who stand alone at the rails of ships, who walk the night streets, who lie in their beds when the hospital grows quiet, when the house is silent, when everyone has gone. "I am the good shepherd; I know my own, and my own know me." "Yea, though I walk through the valley of the shadow, . . ." "For now," wrote Paul, "we see through a glass darkly, but then face to face. Now I know in part; then I shall understand fully, even as I have been fully understood."

Important in these passages is the affirmation that God knows us. The witness is not about how much or how little we know of God —that comes more fully later. Faith *begins* with the affirmation that we are known and that there is nothing hidden: the worst is out— and still we have a Shepherd! To live convinced that God knows us is no small thing.

But there is something more important than knowledge, whether it be the knowledge of buses, of warships and planes, or even of God's knowledge of us. The second thing I learned on the bus that day was that the people there *cared* about what happened. The man with the lunch pail didn't want the boys to be stuck far from home. The heavyset lady didn't want them to face an unbelieving driver in the bus behind. And the lady next to me cared whether our driver, who was new at her job, would make it. Their knowledge of buses was not *the* truth, but their knowledge was placed in the service of truth, and truth was in their caring.

In the South Atlantic, where knowledge is everywhere visible, truth is not. Truth is so absent in the South Atlantic that half the world doesn't know whether to laugh or to weep at the absurdity of it. Weep mostly, I think—in part for those who are dying, but

in part for ourselves at the realization that human beings can be so
knowledgeable and still engage in such stupidity. The people on the
bus would do better. They would understand about pride, and the
importance of preserving it for both countries, and they would find
a way to keep both flags flying. They would do that because they
cared enough about what happened to young soldiers and sailors,
to the Islanders, and even to the sheep. And their caring, whatever
the outcome, would be the lasting truth that would survive the
current debacle in the South Atlantic.

Caring is the central affirmation concerning the Good Shepherd.
Not just that he knows the sheep, which is important, but that he
lays down his life for the sheep, which is crucial. This is no hireling,
no shepherd-for-wages. When the cost of shepherding is greater
than the wages, the hireling flees and leaves the sheep to the wolves.
The Good Shepherd, not being a hireling, gives what wages can
never buy.

But there's more to it than that. This Shepherd is neither British
not Argentinian, neither white nor black, neither first world nor
third world. He always has sheep that are "not of this fold"—and
the longing intention that these other sheep too be equally, and
rightly, cared for.

Truth, wrote Joseph Sittler, frees us from the illusion that knowledge is redemptive. Knowledge makes the buses run; it informs us
about how to get on and off. But truth makes human beings human.
It reaches out to two small boys. Truth suggests transfers from the
trailer. Truth assures the driver that no one will steal the bus.
Truth does not demean a driver for being new, but wishes her well.

Veritas is our motto, but knowledge is our business, and it would
be foolish to deny the importance of knowledge. But once more we
engage in the organized slaughter of human beings, a carnage
enhanced by the use of the latest devices of science, the best our
knowledge can provide. In doing so, we demonstrate that we are
little possessed of truth, that capacity for caring about one another
which is our greatest joy, that which makes us most fully human.
We have made a choice: believing that we are incapable of caring
for and about one another, we have chosen to defend ourselves
with the most deadly devices knowledge can provide—which, in
time of crisis, means that we go to war. Why do we do this? Why

do we believe that we are incapable of caring about one another? Why—when even the people on a bus, also strangers to one another, find it entirely possible to enjoy and practice truth!

Christians, some of us at least, are accused of being naive about human nature and about the so-called inevitability of war. But the issue is precisely at that point—the matter of inevitability. Christians are called precisely in order to see things differently—that is the meaning of repentance. We worship the God who in Christ made the blind see and the deaf hear, who dispossessed demons and taught us to believe that change is possible. We are even enabled to believe that peace is possible, that there are true shepherds and not only hirelings, that a man with a lunch pail is willing to look after the bus.

As Martin Luther might well have said: it is the devil's own device that when the world, like Humpty Dumpty, falls off the wall, each of us runs for cover, locks and bolts the door of our heart, and begins the long involution toward the imprisonment of the self. Knowledgeable about survival, we buy up what we need for the furnishing of our cave, let fall an iron curtain over the window of our souls, and, armed with the defenses of our class, keep watch against those who would invade our prison.

And the truth is not in us.

Truth is a Shepherd who walks in no man's land unafraid and gently rattles the iron curtain at the window of our souls to see if perhaps we won't come out—to walk with him among Humpty Dumpty's pieces and begin to do with compassion and care what all the King's Harriers and all the Junta's soldiers will not be able to do.

He is the truth which frees us from the illusion that knowledge is redemptive.

Truth is in buses.

Can Kindness and Truth Embrace?

MARY LOU KOWNACKI, OSB
Chairperson of the National Council, Pax Christi USA
National Coordinator, Benedictines for Peace

Kindness and truth shall meet. (Ps. 85:11 [NAB])

"Kindness and truth shall embrace." Now there's a love scene worth waiting for.

Too often peace-and-justice zealots like myself get mesmerized by the ascetic figure of John the Baptist striding boldly out of the desert preaching a stern and uncompromising message of truth. Our message is also harsh and, we believe, straight from the mouth of God: get rid of your boat and second car; stop paying war taxes; don't eat meat; quit your job in the nuclear plant! If there's one word we zealots have mastered, it's John's word "Repent!"

A few months ago our community was discussing a passage from Isaiah in which the prophet wrote that rain and snow do not return to the heavens "till they have watered the earth, making it fertile and fruitful" (Isa. 55:10). At the time, our garden was just giving birth to the tomato crop, and so we were full of nature imagery. We spent the time wondering how the soft summer rains had broken up the caked earth and allowed the seed to grow. We contrasted them with the hard and sudden downpours that often flood the ground and drown the seed. Then someone drew a comparison: we peacemakers are often so intense about preaching the truth that we cause more harm than good by trying to force growth where the ground has not been prepared. All of us could relate to the metaphor of trying to clear a straight path for the Lord with dynamite and a bulldozer instead of a pail of water and a hand shovel.

[Delivered December 6, 1981, in Erie, Pennsylvania, to the Benedictine Sisters of Erie. Reprinted by permission from the November 1981 issue of *Sojourners* magazine, 1309 L Street, N. W., Washington, D. C. 20005]

Recently, an example of a sudden downpour on hard ground made national news. When the decision to go ahead with the neutron bomb was announced by President Reagan, Bishop Matthiesen of Amarillo, Texas, issued a statement protesting the decision and calling upon workers at Pantex, the nuclear plant in his diocese, to consider resigning. I was filled with jubilation: rather than another general condemnation of nuclear arms we finally had a specific plan of action.

The next week I read an interview in the *National Catholic Reporter* with one of the "unclean"—a man who works at Pantex and puts the final touches on nuclear bombs. Robert Gutierrez, a 49-year-old Mexican-American who is a deacon in his parish, told the interviewer: "This job is the first good thing I ever had. I quit school after the fourth grade to help support my family, but later earned a GED [general education degree]. . . . If the church thought my job was immoral, why wasn't something said seven years ago when I applied to the diaconate program?" Gutierrez says he can't sleep at night—because he has a family to support and he feels trapped.

Please don't misunderstand, I think Bishop Matthiesen did a brave and prophetic thing, but I also believe Gutierrez and others like him deserve some soft rains.

How can kindness and truth embrace? Well, we could say that for his part Gutierrez should repent and quit his job, and for its part the diocesan church of Amarillo should provide a pastoral program for Pantex workers, plus retraining and a weekly check for the family until Gutierrez finds another job. This would be an ideal enactment of Isaiah's prophetic call to "comfort the people" (Isa. 40:1), a glorious imitation of the God who fondles and nurses us along like a shepherd does newborn lambs (Isa. 40:11). Would that it were all this neat.

Gutierrez is one person and one paycheck. Can the diocese do the same for all 500 Catholics employed at Pantex? How about the tens of thousands involved in the nuclear industry across the country —the scientists, engineers, military personnel, secretaries, and as- sembly plant workers? And that's only one industry. What about the people who earn their living in the multinational corporations that violate human rights? Then think of all the victims of the "truth-filled" statements we've made about abortion, homosexuality, divorce. Imagine all the struggling people caught in sinful situations that they can't break away from. Imagine yourself and me. Thank God for the letter from Peter which reminds us of the infinite patience of God: "He shows you generous patience, since he wants none to perish but all to come to repentance" (2 Pet. 3:9).

If God is so hesitant about calling us to judgment, maybe for our part we could pray: "At times let my passion for truth bend to kindness."

When he was a wise old man Aldous Huxley wrote: "It's a bit embarrassing to have been concerned with human problems all one's life and find at the end that one has no more to offer by way of advice than: 'Try to be a little kinder.'" And it was a Western mystic who said, "Do you want to be a saint? Be kind, be kind, be kind."

To Reach Peace, Teach Peace

MOST REVEREND CARROLL T. DOZIER
Roman Catholic Bishop, Diocese of Memphis, Tennessee

In days to come
    the mount of the Lord's house
Shall be established higher than the mountains;
    it shall rise high above the hills,
And people shall stream to it:
    Many nations shall come, and say,
"Come, let us climb the mount of the Lord,
    to the house of the God of Jacob,
That he may instruct us in his ways,
    that we may walk in his paths."
For from Zion shall go forth instruction,
    and the word of the Lord from Jerusalem.
He shall judge between many peoples
    and impose terms on strong and distant nations;
They shall beat their swords into plowshares,
    and their spears into pruning hooks;
One nation shall not raise the sword against another,
    nor shall they train for war again.
Every man shall sit under his own vine
    or under his own fig tree, undisturbed:
    for the mouth of the Lord of hosts has spoken.
                Mic. 4:1–4 (NAB)

Is there a vision in Israel? If Jesus Christ is the Light of the Nations, and his church the sign and sacrament of a redeemed people that is united with God and all humanity, then what is the Watchman saying when he calls to us from his tower? His is a simple message: "To reach peace" we must "teach peace." That is the message we celebrate today.

Micah's word seems to have anticipated this contemporary

[Delivered January 13, 1979, at the Third Annual World Day of Peace, Detroit]

message, but that is understandable because Micah too was speaking
forth God's word. "The Lord's house," he says, "shall be established
higher than the mountains; it shall rise high above the hills." Is this
not sign? Is it not sacrament also? After all, "people shall stream
to it." If the Lord's house is indeed established "higher than the
mountains," one must be able to see it—and that not only on a
clear day, but also on a day beclouded with confusion and doubt.

If we are to understand peace and teach it, we must begin with
Jesus himself, with what he taught and did. Otherwise, we will have
disobeyed his own injunction and placed the very Light of the
Nations under a bushel basket. Jesus' figure of the lamppost giving
light to all (Matt. 5:15) correlates beautifully with the use of the
word *mountain* by Micah. The good news, the gospel, must not
only exist. It must also be heard—by ears that are open to the
preaching. And it must also be seen—as a sign in the life of that
body which is the church, yes a visible sign, even on a cloudy day.

"Let us climb the mount of the Lord . . . that he may instruct us
in his ways, that we may walk in his paths." Jesus himself, the
Word spoken by the living God, must be ever present to us as the
norm by which we live. His call to us is the call to live daily in his
presence, and by his norms. Unless we dwell upon—and in—this
ever-present reality, accepting his call, we are doomed to obscure
God's Word, to mute his message by filtering it through our own
perspectives, yes our own prejudices.

The Second Vatican Council reminds us forcefully of how we
ourselves can be responsible for the obscuring of the message.
"Atheism," it says, "is not present in the mind of man from the
start. It springs from various causes, among which must be included
a critical *reaction against* religions and, in some places, against the
Christian religion in particular. *Believers* can thus have more than a
little to do with the rise of atheism" (*Gaudium et Spes* #19, emphasis added).

You and I are called to stand for examination and certification
on the subject of God's message to our day. Isaiah uses a similar
figure to make the same point: "Come now, let us talk this over,
says the Lord" (Isa. 1:18). Isaiah makes it sound as if God is
calling his people into a courtroom scene: there will be a hearing!

Micah formulates our public examination quite precisely. He

asks us to score ourselves on this test: "He shall judge between many peoples and impose terms on strong and distant nations; they shall beat their swords into plowshares and their spears into pruning hooks."

In scoring ourselves on this test we must take into account the responsibility we have as persons and our responsibility as church as well. As persons, our own attitude towards violence must be the starting point of our consideration. Has "law and order" become such a mindless slogan that we will countenance any oppression if only it can be subsumed under "law and order?" We need to ask the leaders of our nation: In what direction shall we move? What are the limits to violence? Where will we stand? The Watchman in the tower says: "To reach peace, teach peace."

Our response, to the World Day of Peace is one of testing ourselves by the word of the Lord. We may find it necessary to spend the whole night in prayer and fasting, for unless and until we hear the word of the Lord, we will neither preach it nor do it. If our vision is not illumined by the Lord's own vision, it will never reflect him who is the Light of the Nations. His light takes priority. As 1 John 2:8 puts it: "The night is over; the real light is shining."

There is so much confusion in our daily living. Our culture today is saturated with proferred fulfillments for every desire. It is also filled with fear and discord, anxiety and frustration. We all yearn for the fulfillment promised by Micah: "Every man shall sit under his own vine or under his own fig tree, undisturbed: for the mouth of the Lord of hosts has spoken."

But how shall we arrive at that day of peace? What hinders the coming of peace? What obstacles still block its path?

The obstacle is lack of conversion. We need what Pope Paul VI called "radical conversion, the change of mind and heart." There is special significance for us in the manner in which both John the Baptist and Jesus the Christ first announced the good news. John the precursor taught, "Reform your lives! The reign of God is at hand!" (Matt. 3:2). Later, "when he [Jesus] heard that John had been arrested, he withdrew to Galilee. . . . From that time on Jesus began to proclaim this theme: Reform your lives! The kingdom of heaven is at hand" (Matt. 4:12, 17). Mark's Gospel reports the same matter in this way: "After John's arrest, Jesus appeared in

Galilee proclaiming the good news of God: This is the time of fulfillment. The reign of God is at hand! Reform your lives and believe in the gospel!" (Mark 1:14–15).

The reign or kingdom which John and Jesus both proclaimed had long been in the mainstream of Jewish thought and hope. The good news was clearly described already in the sixty-fifth chapter of Isaiah: "Lo, I am about to create new heavens and a new earth; the things of the past shall not be remembered, or come to mind" (v. 17). "None shall hurt or destroy on all my holy mountain, says the Lord" (v. 25). Because the time long promised was near, indeed already at hand, the need for reformation was immediate and pressing. John and Jesus both called for it: "Reform your lives . . ."

Our present moment of history calls for that same reformation. Pope Paul VI posed the question in the beginning of his exhortation on Evangelization: "In our day, what has happened to that hidden energy of the good news which is able to have a powerful effect on one's conscience?" The question is whether God's word has lost its power *or* we have failed to reform our lives.

If it is indeed necessary to teach peace in order to reach peace, then we must first in all honesty ask ourselves: Do we believe in the "energy of the good news"? Do we believe in the reign of God now? The questions themselves point to the need for conversion. "Each individual gains the kingdom and salvation through a total interior renewal which the gospel calls *metanoia*—a radical conversion, a profound change of mind and heart" (*Evangelization in the Modern World* #10).

The good news has been compromised in our culture. We do not seem to understand that the call to the reign of God, the call to the kingdom of God, the call to discipleship is in fact the call to live now in that kingdom and under that reign. To do this it is absolutely necessary to reform, to change radically in mind and heart.

One clue to our living now in the kingdom of God, under the reign of God, is that we begin to grasp the importance of human rights in our life together. We cannot fulfill our citizenship in God's kingdom unless we are aware of the equality of all God's children. Human rights accepted and lived out are the heart of the Fatherhood of God and the sister-brotherhood of God's people. "It is Christ Jesus who is our peace, and who made the two of us one by breaking down the barrier of hostility that kept us apart" (Eph. 2:14).

Pope John Paul II recently wrote to the Secretary General of the United Nations Kurt Waldheim on the thirtieth anniversary of the Universal Declaration of Human Rights: "In the world as we find it today, what criteria can we use to see that the rights of all persons are protected? What basis can we offer as the soil in which individual and social rights might grow? Unquestionably that basis is the dignity of the human person. Pope John XXIII explained this in *Pacem in Terris*: "Any well regulated and profitable association of men and women in society demands acceptance of one fundamental principle: that each individual is truly a person. . . . As such he or she has rights and duties which together flow as a direct consequence of his or her nature. These rights and duties are universal and inviolable and therefore altogether inalienable."

Radical conversion, then, and an understanding of human rights and of our responsibility to live daily in the reign of God are the principles we must teach if we are to reach peace. But even these can remain abstract unless we learn of their concreteness—again in the words of Jesus. Remember how Jesus answered the questions put to him by the disciples of the imprisoned John the Baptist: "Go back and report to John what you see and hear: The blind recover their sight, cripples walk, lepers are cured, the deaf hear, dead men are raised to life, and the poor have the good news preached to them. Blest is the man who finds no stumbling block in me" (Matt. 11:4–6).

These words are very practical. They speak of concrete things. They give us specific signs of Jesus' presence—actions that characterize life under the reign of God. Here is indeed the new creation of which Isaiah spoke.

In these words, yes in these deeds we see how radical is the conversion we need, how much our minds and hearts have yet to change. The concreteness of the kingdom is shocking. Simeon's prophecy that Jesus would be a sign of contradiction, of rising and falling, Simeon's reference to a piercing sword (Luke 2:34–35) was never truer than it is today. Truly Jesus' kingdom of good news for the poor and suffering is "not of this world." The contradiction stands plainly before us: in the words of Micah, will it be swords or plowshares? The alternatives are clear, the choices concrete.

Salt II is spoken of as an arms "limitation" treaty and citizens regard it as the beginning in a disarmament process. But if we accept Salt II we in fact add *more* weapons to our arsenal, and the plowshares so desperately needed by the human family are turned into swords. Defense Secretary Harold Brown says: "Even with Salt II we will have to increase the present rate of defense spending just in order to maintain essential equivalence." General David Jones, Chairman of the Joint Chiefs of Staff, says that they will support the Salt II agreement "only if we can proceed with the program necessary to allow essential equivalence." By "essential equivalence" Brown and Jones means that the U.S. nuclear striking force must be kept in approximate balance with that of the Soviet Union, not only in numbers but also in effectiveness.

Now here is the sign of contradiction. The entire effect of that arsenal is to kill, blind, cripple, maim, and hurt. Compare that with the effects to which Jesus pointed when he said, "Go back and report to John what you see" (Matt. 11:4).

You and I must make a concrete decision—at stake is our *metanoia*. Which of the two alternatives reflect the requirements of the reign of God? Either we stand with the arsenal of equivalent destruction, or we stand naked and defenseless except for the power of our God.

Here then is the primary step, the first decision we must make if we are to teach peace. There is no other way. Our distraction with philosophical explanations of war and even with the "just-war theory" has been the source of much violence throughout the history of Christendom. The challenge today is to start anew, and be concrete.

Personal conversion means a reconciling life. Our individual lives must be so lived that they manifest a harmony of relationship with all of our brothers and sisters. We must leave behind grudge and prejudice. We must overcome evil with good, forsaking violence in thought, word, and deed.

Conversion must bring back a vision, one with all the newness of Isaiah's vision. We can set ourselves a goal for the year 2000. We might call it the Jubilee Year, as in the Book of Leviticus: "This year you shall make sacred by proclaiming liberty in the land for all its inhabitants. It shall be a jubilee for you, when every one of you shall return to his own property, every one to his own family estate" (Lev. 25:10). Our platform for peace need not be intricate.

It might ask every nation to reduce its armaments annually by 5 percent—until they reach zero in the year 2000. Then everyone would indeed "sit under their own vine or under their own fig tree, undisturbed."

The effort should be undertaken ecumenically. The Book of Leviticus would afford an excellent starting point for both Christians and Jews. Our fervor and our honesty in dialogue would, with God's help, gather others into the pilgrimage of peace towards Jubilee.

There would be a role for the youth of the country too, wherever they are in their education. I would remind them of the request of Pope John Paul II that they learn foreign languages so that they can be our interpreters and make communication easier across frontiers as we publish our call for a Jubilee Year, and that they prepare for lives of disinterested service to countries with the fewest resources. Ecumenically, the Mennonites, the American Friends, and the Church of the Brethren have already shown the way.

We must strike down the contradictory signs that equate God's reign and kingdom with the powers of this world. We need the courage to change even our schools—wherever they project a military viewpoint by holding high the sword rather than the plowshare.

These are only some of the steps that could lead us year by year towards the renewed understanding of this world as God's gift to all his children, given so that all might live together in unity and love. When we focus on the things Jesus said and did, our conversion will show us more clearly the concrete path ahead. "My command is this—that you love one another." We begin by doing that today, in concrete ways.

Pope John Paul II closed his message on the World Day of Peace with these words of hope: "To everyone, Christians, believers, and men and women of good will, I say: Do not be afraid to take a chance on peace, to teach peace. The human aspiration for peace will not be disappointed forever. Our work for peace, inspired by that love which does not pass away, will surely produce its fruits. Peace will be the last word of history."

A Very Sad Story

TAZU SHIBAMA
Survivor, Hiroshima

My name is Tazu Shibama from Hiroshima. I come here to tell you my story. I am very happy to have this occasion.

When I came over to Los Angeles three weeks ago, many people came to me and said: "Tazu, where did you learn your English?" So I said: "When I was twelve years old my father put me into a Methodist Church–supported mission school. There I learned my first English. When I finished the high school course, Miss Gaines, my dear missionary teacher, said, 'Tazu, if you get teacher training, you will become a good teacher,' and she arranged for me to go to Nashville, Tennessee, to the George Peabody College for Teachers. It was 1930, fifty years ago."

I finished my training and went back to that same school where Miss Gaines was—Hiroshima Girls' High School. When the bomb came I was a teacher and it was hot summer time, but students did not get any summer vacation because the war was going on and there were seven hundred girls in that school at that time.

They were divided into two groups. The older ones—16, 17, 18—were taken out of town to go to the military factory to help make the army supplies. So they were not in town. The younger ones—13, 14, and 15—remained in the city and went to school to learn. I was ordered to look after those younger ones. That's why I was in town and had the bombing experience.

I will tell you what happened on that day. At 8:15 the bomb was dropped on top of Hiroshima, but there was no warning so we did not know what really happened because the bomb exploded but did not give any sound to us. Of course there was a big sound of explo-

[Delivered April 13, 1980, at the Peace Sabbath, the Riverside Church, New York]

sion, but the sound was too big that our ears could not catch. My father was out of Hiroshima city. He said he and people over there heard a big bang but all the people in Hiroshima city did not hear any sound at all. We only saw a sort of yellowish flash and the next moment everybody was crushed underneath the broken house.

All the Japanese houses were blown up and fell on us in small pieces and covered us up. In that way, I was buried in that nest thinking, oh, here in this darkness I must be dying. But in about ten minutes' time I had all my family sent into the country and I was all by myself there. There was somebody else in that house where I was buried. It happened to be my next-door neighbor. He was standing fifty yards away from me. When the bomb came the blast blew him and buried him beside me. He was strong enough to make his way out and helped me out, and I'm sorry to say he lost his wife and two daughters. He couldn't save them.

Well, then when I came to the streets I was very much surprised. There was no Hiroshima city in front of me. Thousands and thousands of houses all blown down and flattened. Many people were walking in miserable condition—that is, those people walking in the street at that time exposed to the radiation. Some people of course were killed immediately. Some of them who were strong enough to walk, they were walking in the streets in thousands but their hairs were all burned, their faces were burned, skin hanging down, their shirts and pants all burnt and dropped off. Some of the boys had only belts around; some of the girls maybe a pair of shoes, that's all.

They walked in silence.

The shock was so great that they lost words—nobody spoke. They were hurrying in silence just like ghosts or like shadows and even their little children did not cry. They were all hurrying to get out of this terrible place.

They were facing to the Hiroshima station, so I followed them to go to my father's place in the country, to get a train out of Hiroshima station. Before we came to the station there was a river and we had to cross a bridge. Of course there was a big concrete bridge and many people went that way but there was another small wooden bridge behind it and I knew it would give the nearest cut to the station so I took that small bridge. I was walking barefooted and I was surprised it was so hot. Well some of the parts of the bridge were already started burning. It was about thirty minutes after the blast but already burning and so hot. I had to run across the bridge. Well underneath the water was running and I just could not understand why this bridge is burning. There is no fire to start it, but the bomb gave that terrific heat that started the fire.

In thirty minutes' time many of the Japanese student houses started burning and in one day the whole Hiroshima city was burnt down to ashes. Well my students, three hundred fifty of them, some of them were playing in the school yard. They were exposed to the radiation immediately and killed. Many of them stayed in the school house. They were crushed underneath the broken house. They couldn't get out and fire killed them all. In that way, I lost eighteen teachers and three hundred fifty of my good students.

That is a very sad story.

Well I was very lucky to be able to survive because in that afternoon I walked ten miles north of Hiroshima where my father was, where he gave me good food to eat. I had fresh air to breathe, fresh water to drink, fresh vegetables such as tomatoes, cucumbers, and eggs, and so on that built my health back again. It took me just one year to be able to work again but I was one of the very, very lucky ones to be able to survive. Because some of the people living may have been one week or two weeks in Hiroshima city. They did not go away from the city because they had to look for the missing members of their family. When they stayed in Hiroshima, the air was bad, water was poison, and they had very little food to eat— that's why they had leukemia, the blood disease. They lost their hair, their gums started bleeding and never stopped, and they died in terrific suffering, high temperatures. So Hiroshima lost 200 thousand of the people there, that is, two-thirds of the whole population of that city at that time.

Well it is not a happy story to tell you, but my friends, my students, my relatives they all died. I am sure they have some message to tell but they cannot speak. They have no mouth to speak and I am one of the very lucky ones to be able to survive and must carry the message for their sake. That's why I am here, because I can speak a little English and I will carry my message to you: Wars are no good. Weapons, no matter how big and strong they are, they do not give us good answers for our questions.

Only peace and love give us happiness. Thank you.

Faith and Disarmament

RAYMOND G. HUNTHAUSEN
Roman Catholic Archbishop of Seattle

If anyone wants to be a follower of mine, let that person renounce self and take up the cross and follow me. For anyone who wants to save one's own life will lose it; but anyone who loses one's life for my sake, and for the sake of the gospel, will save it.

Mark 8:34–35

I am grateful for having been invited to speak to you on disarmament because it forces me to a kind of personal disarmament. This is a subject I have thought about and prayed over for many years. I can vividly recall hearing the news of the atomic bombing of Hiroshima in 1945. I was deeply shocked. I could not then put into words the shock I felt from the news that a city of hundreds of thousands of people had been devastated by a single bomb. Hiroshima challenged my faith as a Christian in a way I am only now beginning to understand. That awful event and its successor at Nagasaki sank into my soul, as they have in fact sunk into the souls of all of us, whether we recognize it or not.

I am sorry to say that I did not speak out against the evil of nuclear weapons until many years later. I was especially challenged on the issue by an article I read in 1976 by Jesuit Father Richard McSorley titled "It's a Sin to Build a Nuclear Weapon." Father McSorley wrote: "The taproot of violence in our society today is our intention to use nuclear weapons. Once we have agreed to that, all other evil is minor in comparison. Until we squarely face the question of our consent to use nuclear weapons, any hope of large-scale improvement of public morality is doomed to failure." I agree.

[Delivered June 12, 1981, to the Pacific Northwest Synod of the Lutheran Church in America, meeting at Pacific Lutheran University in Tacoma, Washington]

Our willingness to destroy life everywhere on this earth, for the sake of our security as Americans, is at the root of many other terrible events in our country.

I was also challenged to speak out against nuclear armament by the nearby construction of the Trident submarine base and by the first-strike nuclear doctrine which Trident represents. The nuclear warheads fired from one Trident submarine will be able to destroy as many as 408 separate areas, each with a bomb five times more powerful than the one used at Hiroshima. One Trident submarine has the destructive equivalent of 2,040 Hiroshima bombs. Trident and other new weapons systems, such as the MX and cruise missiles, have such extraordinary accuracy and explosive power that they can only be understood as a buildup to a first-strike capability. First-strike nuclear weapons are immoral and criminal. They benefit only the arms corporations and the insane dreams of those who wish to "win" a nuclear holocaust.

I was also moved to speak out against Trident because it is being based here. We must take special responsibility for what is in our own backyard. And when crimes are being prepared in our name, we must speak plainly. I say with a deep consciousness of these words that Trident is the Auschwitz of Puget Sound.

Father McSorley's article and the local basing of Trident are what awakened me to a new sense of the gospel call to peacemaking in the nuclear age. They brought back the shock of Hiroshima. Since that reawakening five years ago, I have tried to respond in both a more prayerful and more vocal way than I did in 1945. I feel the need to respond by prayer because our present crisis goes far deeper than politics. I have heard many perceptive political analyses of the nuclear situation, but their common element is despair. It is no wonder. The nuclear arms race can sum up in a few final moments the violence of tens of thousands of years, raised to an almost infinite power—a demonic reversal of the Creator's power of giving life. But politics is itself powerless to overcome the demonic in its midst. It needs another dimension. I am convinced that a way out of this terrible crisis can be discovered by our deepening in faith and prayer, so that we learn to rely for our security not on missiles but on the loving care of that One who gives and sustains life. We need to return to the gospel with open hearts to learn once again what it is to have faith.

We are told by Our Lord: "Blessed are the peacemakers: they shall be called children of God." The gospel calls us to be peacemakers, to practice a divine way of reconciliation. But the next beatitude in Matthew's sequence implies that peacemaking may also be blessed because the persecution that it provokes is the further way into the kingdom: "Blessed are those who are persecuted in the cause of right; theirs is the kingdom of heaven."

To understand today the gospel call to peacemaking, and its consequence, persecution, I want to refer especially to these words of Our Lord in Mark: "If anyone wants to be a follower of mine, let that person renounce self and take up the cross and follow me. For anyone who wants to save one's own life will lose it; but anyone who loses one's life for my sake, and for the sake of the gospel, will save it." Scripture scholars tell us that these words lie at the very heart of Mark's Gospel, in his watershed passage on the meaning of faith in Christ. The point of Jesus' teaching here is inescapable: as his followers, we cannot avoid the cross given to each one of us. I am sorry to have to remind myself—and each of you—that by "the cross" Jesus was referring to the means by which the Roman Empire executed those whom it considered revolutionaries. Jesus' first call in the gospel is to love of God and of one's neighbor. But when he gives flesh to that commandment by the more specific call to the cross, I am afraid that like most of you I prefer to think in abstract terms, not in the specific context in which Our Lord lived and died. Jesus' call to the cross was a call to love God and one's neighbor in so direct a way that the authorities in power could only regard it as subversive and revolutionary. "Taking up the cross," "losing one's life" meant being willing to die at the hands of political authorities for the truth of the gospel, for that love of God in which we are all one.

As followers of Christ we need to take up our cross in the nuclear age. I believe that one obvious meaning of the cross is unilateral disarmament. Jesus' acceptance of the cross—rather than the sword raised in his defense—is the gospel's statement of unilateral disarmament. We are called to follow. Our security as people of faith lies not in demonic weapons which threaten all life on earth. Our security is in a loving, caring God. We must dismantle our weapons of terror and place our reliance on God.

I am told by some that unilateral disarmament in the face of atheistic Communism is insane. I find myself observing that nuclear *armament* by anyone is itself atheistic, and anything but sane. I am also told that the choice of unilateral disarmament is a political impossibility in this country. If so, perhaps the reason is that we have forgotten what it would be like to act out of faith. But I speak here of that choice not as a political platform—it might not win elections —but as a moral imperative for followers of Christ. A choice has been put before us: anyone who wants to save one's own life by nuclear arms will lose it; but anyone who loses one's life by giving up those arms for Jesus' sake, and for the sake of the gospel of love, will save it.

To ask one's country to relinquish its security in arms is to encourage risk—a more reasonable risk than constant nuclear escalation, but a risk nevertheless. I am struck by how much more terrified we Americans often are by talk of disarmament than by the march to nuclear war. We whose nuclear arms terrify millions around the globe are terrified by the thought of being without them. Our nation without such power would feel naked. To relinquish our hold on global destruction would seem like we were risking everything, and it would be risking everything—but in a direction opposite to the way in which we now risk everything. Nuclear arms protect privilege and exploitation. Giving them up would mean having to give up our economic power over other peoples. Peace and justice go together. On the path we now follow, our economic policies toward other countries require nuclear weapons. Giving up the weapons would mean giving up more than our means of global terror. It would mean giving up the reason for such terror—our privileged place in the world.

How can such a process—of taking up the cross of nonviolence— happen in a country where our government seems paralyzed by the arms corporations? In a country where many of the citizens, perhaps most of the citizens, are numbed into passivity by the very magnitude and complexity of the issue, while being horrified by the prospect of nuclear holocaust? Clearly some action is demanded—some form of nonviolent resistance. Some people may choose to write to their elected representatives at the national and state level, others may choose to take part in marches, demonstrations, or similar forms of protest. Obviously there are many ways that action can be taken.

I would like to share a vision of still another action that could be taken: a sizeable number of people—five thousand, ten thousand, a half million people—refusing to pay 50 percent of their taxes as an act of nonviolent resistance to nuclear murder and suicide. I think that would be a definite step toward disarmament. Our paralyzed political process needs the catalyst of nonviolent action based on faith. We have to refuse to give incense—in our day, tax dollars— to our nuclear idol. On April 15 we can vote for unilateral disarmament with our lives. Form 1040 is the place where the Pentagon enters all of our lives, and asks our unthinking cooperation with the idol of nuclear destruction. I think the teaching of Jesus tells us to render to a nuclear-armed Caesar what that Caesar deserves—tax resistance—and to begin to render to God alone that complete trust which we now give, through our tax dollars, to a demonic form of power. Some would call what I am urging "civil disobedience." I prefer to see it as obedience to God.

I fully realize that many will disagree with my position on uni- lateral disarmament and tax resistance. I also realize that one can argue endlessly about specific tactics, but no matter how we differ on tactics, one thing at least is certain: we must demand over and over again that our political leaders make peace and disarmament, not war and increased armaments, their first priority. We must demand that time and effort and money be placed first of all toward efforts to let everyone know that the United States is primarily interested *not* in being the strongest military power on earth, but in being the strongest peace advocate. We must challenge every politician who talks endlessly about building up our arms and never about efforts for peace. We must ask our people to question their government when it concentrates its efforts on shipping arms to countries that need food, when it accords the military an open checkbook while claiming that assistance to the poor must be slashed in the name of balancing the budget, when it devotes most of its time and energy and money to developing war strategy and not peace strategy.

Creativity is always in short supply. This means that it must be used for the most valuable purposes. Yet it seems evident that most of our creative efforts are not going into peace but into war. We have too many people who begin with the premise that little can be done to arrange for a decrease in arms spending because the Soviet

Union is bent on bankrupting itself on armaments no matter what we do. We have too few people who are willing to explore every possible path to decreasing armaments.

In our Catholic Archdiocese of Seattle I have recommended to our people that we all turn more intently to the Lord this year in response to the escalation of nuclear arms, and that we do so especially by fasting and prayer on Monday of each week. That is the way, I believe, to depend on a power far greater than the hydrogen bomb. I believe that only by turning our lives around in the most fundamental ways, submitting ourselves to the infinite love of God, will we be given the vision and strength to take up the cross of nonviolence.

The nuclear arms race can be stopped. Nuclear weapons can be abolished. *That* I believe with all my heart and faith, my sisters and brothers. The key to that nuclear-free world is the cross at the center of the gospel, and our response to it. The terrible responsibility which you and I have in this nuclear age is to make real the faith we profess—in a God who in the person of Jesus Christ has transformed death into life. Our faith sees the transformation of death, through the cross of suffering love, as an ongoing process. That process is our way into hope of a new world.

Jesus made it clear that the cross and empty tomb didn't end with him. Thank God they didn't. We are living in a time when new miracles are needed, when a history threatened by overwhelming death needs resurrection by Almighty God. God alone is our salvation, through a nonviolent cross of suffering love accepted by each of us. Let us call on the Holy Spirit to move us all into that nonviolent action which will take us to our own cross, and to the new earth beyond.

A Dream (Sometime in the Future...)

JIM WALLIS
Founder and Pastor, the Sojourners community, Washington, D. C.
Editor, *Sojourners* magazine

Blessed are the peacemakers, for they shall be called sons of God.
Matt. 5:9

The government is worried. Used to be that the churches were
satisfied with just issuing statements and declarations on world
peace. Everyone knew that such pronouncements didn't mean much:
church members were as scared of "the Russians" as everybody else.
Christians too wanted to hang onto the life style to which they had
grown accustomed. They were as glad for the nuclear arsenal as the
rest of us, no matter what their leaders at denominational headquar-
ters were saying.

Anyway, the church leaders too had money invested in the big
weapons companies. They paid their war taxes, and they fought for
power and influence just as hard as all the other lobbying groups in
Washington. The only real difference between the church lobbies and
the National Rifle Association was that churches couldn't deliver
their constituency.

That was before it all happened. They say it's a revival—just like
what happened more than a hundred years ago when a lot of Christians turned against slavery. Whatever it is, it's got the government
worried.

Evangelists are springing up all over. They're preaching the gospel
and saying that our country's nuclear policy is a sin—a *sin,* mind
you, not merely a social or political problem.

It's idolatry, they say, to put our own nation ahead of the lives of

[Delivered on Memorial Day, 1980, at the Peace Pentecost in Washington,
D. C.]

89

millions of other people. They're going all over the country saying that to turn to Jesus means to turn away from nuclear weapons.

Christians are no longer happy just to give good advice to the government about international cooperation. They say they must first put their own house in order. Pastors are telling their people that the Lord wants them to quit supporting the arms race. And the people are quitting.

They're calling it repentance. Engineers, businesspersons, and workers have formed groups to pray for peace and to study the Bible on peace. They're telling their employers that they will no longer help to make nuclear weapons and that they will quit their jobs if the companies continue making them.

This is presenting quite a problem for management. Many of these repentant Christians are in key positions. And even after they quit or are fired, they keep coming back to talk to the other employees. Evangelism, they call it.

Christian researchers, scientists, and professors are saying that their God-given responsibility is to save lives and protect the earth, not to destroy creation. They are refusing to work on military projects.

Even in the military, Christian service personnel are saying they won't use nuclear weapons. Many are leaving the military altogether. Armed forces chaplains have been relieved of their duties after giving sermons on the need for peace.

For years, the Pentagon itself has been honeycombed with prayer groups. But never before have the group members talked or prayed about their work. They thought politics should be kept out of prayer. Now they claim that their faith is causing them to examine their jobs. Many of the Christians on the inside are beginning to join the protesting Christians on the outside. They are vowing never to return to their former work.

There were always a few Christians here and there who wouldn't pay their war taxes. But now by the thousands they are deciding that taxes for war are not part of what they should render to Caesar. Churches are holding workshops on tax resistance right after the Sunday-school hour.

Most startling of all is the way Christians are converging on nuclear sites all over the country. They call it moving the geography of worship and prayer. What better place to confess their faith in the true

God, they ask, than at the altars and idols of the false gods?

No nuclear facility, military base, or weapons plant is spared the regular presence of Christians, especially on important dates in the religious calendar and, remembering Hiroshima and Nagasaki, on August 6 and 9. Whole congregations have come out. They call it their peace ministry.

Many of these Christians have been arrested and charged with illegal entry. But they go back and do it again. They say it helps to make visible what the government wants to keep invisible; it helps to make public what has been hidden from view.

And that's causing problems in the jails. These Christians go on having their Bible studies and prayer meetings behind bars. Some of them say that's the best place to have them. Other inmates are joining them, and some new groups are forming called "Prisoners for Peace." Even some of the guards have gotten involved.

There's trouble with Christian police who don't want to arrest their fellow Christians. A judge recently broke down in tears, right in the courtroom; he said he would no longer convict anyone for protesting nuclear weapons. A prosecutor out West has dropped charges against some Christians who were praying at a nuclear weapons plant—and filed charges against the plant for violating international law by making weapons of total destruction.

Some of the churches have even been making contact with churches in the Soviet Union—bypassing all proper diplomatic channels. They say that Soviet Christians too belong to the body of Christ. They claim their bonds with Christians in the Soviet Union are stronger than their loyalty to their own country. Maybe, they say, if U.S. and Soviet Christians started to act like brothers and sisters, their governments might wake up.

Finally, they have told the government that it must stop the arms race. Just stop, they say. They vow to withhold all political support from any public official who will not promise to do that.

All this has happened because Christians have the idea that their faith is tied up in this nuclear thing. It was a lot easier when they regarded nuclear war as a political issue, turned it over to a committee and held educational seminars on it. Now they meet to worship about it, pray over it, and act like their faith is at stake in it all. They say that to follow Jesus is to be a peacemaker.

The idea is spreading. And the government is worried.

Pax Romana and Pax Christi

DOROTHEE SOELLE
Professor of Theology, Union Theological Seminary, New York

In those days a decree went out from Caesar Augustus that all the world should be enrolled. This was the first enrollment, when Quirinius was governor of Syria. And all went to be enrolled, each to his own city. And Joseph also went up from Galilee, from the city of Nazareth, to Judea, to the city of David, which is called Bethlehem, because he was of the house and lineage of David, to be enrolled with Mary, his betrothed, who was with child. And while they were there, the time came for her to be delivered. And she gave birth to her first-born son and wrapped him in swaddling cloths, and laid him in a manger, because there was no place for them in the inn.

And in that region there were shepherds out in the field, keeping watch over their flock by night. And an angel of the Lord appeared to them, and the glory of the Lord shone around them, and they were filled with fear. And the angel said to them, "Be not afraid; for behold, I bring you good news of a great joy which will come to all the people; for to you is born this day in the city of David a Savior, who is Christ the Lord. And this will be a sign for you: you will find a babe wrapped in swaddling cloths and lying in a manger." And suddenly there was with the angel a multitude of the heavenly host praising God and saying, "Glory to God in the highest, and on earth peace among men with whom he is pleased!"

Luke 2:1–14

People talk a lot these days about peace. The New Testament too has much to say about peace. But there is a distinction between the two different kinds of peace, a distinction that shows up already in Luke's story of the birth of Jesus.

In the very first part of this Christmas Gospel we hear about the

---

[Delivered in December 1981 in James Memorial Chapel, Union Theological Seminary, New York]

decree of Caesar Augustus that all the world should be enrolled for purposes of taxation. To be in compliance Joseph and Mary have to travel from Nazareth to Bethlehem for the general registration. This legal measure was designed to exploit the subjugated inhabitants of the Roman provinces and keep them under the control of the Roman emperor. The Roman administration had to identify the people in these provinces and register them in order to get a hold on them and tax them and induct them.

The enrollment measure was part of a complex and encompassing system called the Pax Romana—the peace of Rome. This system consisted of a world order in which there was a center (Rome) and a periphery (the conquered provinces). In the geopolitical center of this world order there was material abundance and an unending quest for new commodities and pleasures, but also moral corruption, psychic emptiness, and a pervasive lack of human feeling. On the outer edges of this same order, out in the dominated provinces, there was at the same time unbelievable misery—people lacking in food, water, shelter, work, and education; apathetic hopelessness was also widespread among the impoverished masses. Their economic situation is clearly reflected in the hired workers, mentioned in Jesus' Parable of the Vineyard (Matt. 20:1–16), who stand in line all day long just waiting to be hired. Many other texts of the New Testament also talk about the landless masses and about their hunger, their diseases, and their lack of possessions.

Historically, the setting of all these stories is the Pax Romana, the Roman Peace, a system that was built on domination of the impoverished. It was a highly sophisticated and well-oiled system, so constituted that the rich would become richer and the poor poorer. The whole arrangement was called Peace—the Pax Romana—by those who loved it and profited from it!

But the story in Luke 2 talks also about a different peace, one that is specifically announced as good news to the poor. "Peace on earth" in the angelic message does not mean simply peace later—in heaven after this life is over; it does not mean simply peace with God—deep down inside your own individual soul. It means rather Pax Christi, the Peace of Christ that begins here and now with the poor who have long since buried their hopes. This different peace is the peace that leads the shepherds from hopelessness and fear into a "great joy which will come to all the people." Pax Christi is the good news for all who suffer under the Pax Romana. It is news addressed to the fringes, news that eventually will reach to the center as well.

This other peace, which is not built upon oppression and military domination, leads the people who seek it into persecution—because the two kinds of peace are in conflict. The messengers of Christ's peace either are not listened to, or they are persecuted, silenced, and if necessary eliminated by the state police—as Paul was. The Roman system has many ways to silence people and make them believe in the Pax Romana. Some of the methods emerge clearly from the background of the Christmas story, which reports, for example, the fiscal policies of the Roman government. Caesar Augustus and Pontius Pilate stand at the beginning and at the end of the Jesus story: the Pax Romana is a kind of frame for the Pax Christi. Specialists in enrollment, taxation, and torture serve as the official representatives of the Roman power. Theirs is an organized system of violence, complete with the militarism that was necessary to exploit the provinces and maintain the luxury of the powerful few in the center.

These, then, are two very different concepts of peace—the Pax Romana and the Pax Christi, the military peace that builds on intimidation through a bureaucracy, and the other peace that prevails among people with whom God is pleased, especially the poor. The two are quite different, and one cannot understand the New Testament without keeping in mind the distinction. Pax Romana and Pax Christi are mutually exclusive. We cannot have both. We cannot have the peace of Christ in our hearts, for our inner selves, while depending on the Pax Romana to guarantee our external life style and the world order in which we live.

When I first began to learn about history, the textbooks and teachers spoke about the glories and beauty of the Pax Romana. No one in our schools told us about the blind, the lame, the crippled, and the sick—mentioned on almost every page of the New Testament—who peopled that same world. Our whole educational system simply echoed the Roman propagandists who called the subjugation of other people "peace," the exploitation of the weak "order," and those who opposed the system "terrorists." But terror was in reality a major means for perpetuating this sort of "peace." Any "peace" built on militarism is in effect a terrorist operation—it works through terror. Terroristic threats and actions are what make it effective. The permanent preparation for war, the readiness to kill, is called in strategic terms "deterrence," but notice how in the very center of that word *deterrence* there is embedded the word *terror*. Caesar's means for keeping the world under Roman domination included tax policy, economic dictatorship, administered pricing, and counter-insurgency, including torture, interrogation, and militarism. The Pax Romana was a terrorist system. For the majority of the people living in the whole known world of that time, it meant a subsistence level of existence in a never-ending daily struggle for survival.

If we look around our own world today, we easily see that there is a war going on right now—the war between rich and poor. By even the most modest estimates this war is producing worldwide about fifteen thousand casualties each day—fifteen thousand people killed by quenchable hunger and curable disease. The bombs and missiles we produce in the name of "defense preparedness" are already falling on the poor—right now!

In the old days the historian propagandists called the Roman system of domination "peace." We even find the word inscribed on ancient Roman coins, where Caesar is termed a "peacemaker." This is the word that Jesus deliberately picked up. He took it away from those who in his day were misusing it and gave it to people who work and live for a wholly different kind of system and order. "Blessed are the peacemakers," Jesus said—to women, and fisherfolk, and other forgotten people! And when he said it, it was not the Pax Romana he had in mind. For Jesus, peacebuilding did not include terrorizing people through military buildups and maneuvers. It had to do rather with human reconciliation and well-being, beginning with the lowliest and least.

Pax Christi, the peace of Christ, is different from the Pax Romana. It is built not on militarism but on justice. There is no other way truly to have peace. We have to choose which kind of peace we will seek and work for.

O God, Father of the Prince of Peace, look with patience as well as judgment on those who feed the fires of war. Let nothing hide from us the terror, the tragedy, the despair of war, nor let our honorable motives cover the blasphemy against thy love in every injury and every death visited upon men, women, and children in the name of high principle or national defense. O Lord, may we be servants of your peace, not only by our opinions but also by our actions; through Jesus Christ our Lord, who took upon himself our violence that we might have peace in our hearts and in our world. Amen.

Adapted from *Prayers for Worship Leaders*
by Arnold Kenseth and Richard P. Unsworth